Classroom Questions

WHAT KINDS?

Norris M. Sanders

Director of Research
Manitowoc Public Schools
Manitowoc, Wisconsin

Harper & Row

Publishers · New York

CLASSROOM QUESTIONS: WHAT KINDS?

Library of Congress Catalog Card Number: 66–10841

CONTENTS

EDITOR'S INTRODUCTION

QUESTIONS HAVE ALWAYS BEEN the major stock in trade for teachers. At all levels, students are plied with different kinds of inquiries. Throughout his academic career, questions, both oral and written, exert a major influence upon the student. In some cases, the future professional activities of the student will reflect the results of examinations.

Traditionally, questions have been used to determine what has been *learned*—too often as isolated bits of knowledge which are of little value. Thus, there is a wide range in the quality of questions. Some of the elements which make a good question are: precision, clarity and close connection to the matters on which the question is based.

There is marked difference in the competence of teachers in the art of questioning. As stated by Dr. Sanders, the teachers most talented in questioning are usually deep and continuing scholars. Good questions recognize the wide possibilities of thought and are built around varying forms of thinking. Good questions are directed toward learning and evaluative thinking, rather than determining what has been *learned* in a narrow sense.

Classroom Questions has enjoyed some five years of field development and evaluation in the public schools of Manitowoc, Wisconsin. The author has held seminars on questions with some 40 groups, including teachers in various public school systems, professional education organizations, and college groups.

This book should be of great assistance to those who make and ask classroom questions. It is my belief that it will also reduce the perplexity of those taking examinations. Even more important, *Classroom Questions* will help students develop more effective and diversified thinking which should prove valuable not only in their student days but, indeed, throughout their lives.

June, 1965   JOHN GUY FOWLKES

PREFACE

IT IS A COMMON COMPLAINT among teachers that the main obstacle
to the solution of the problems of education is lack of time. In the
summer of 1959 the Wisconsin Improvement Program, under
the leadership of Dr. John Guy Fowlkes, gave over one hundred
teachers from eight school systems a unique opportunity: we
were given the resources of the University of Wisconsin, con-
sultant services from many of the most creative educators in the
nation, and living expenses; but, most important, we were given
time to think and plan and do. The ideas in this book germinated
and grew in the Wisconsin Improvement Program, and I hope
they present testimony that Dr. Fowlkes' confidence in us was
not misplaced.

The most active center for the study of questions has been in
the public schools in Manitowoc, Wisconsin. Teachers in four
summer workshops worked to develop new ideas in the area of
questions. The program would have been impossible without
the encouragement and leadership of Superintendent Angus
Rothwell, Superintendent Charles Jones, and the Manitowoc
Board of Education.

A note of appreciation is due to my department chairman,
Newton Jones, and to my colleagues on an instructional team in

Problems of Democracy, Ruth Fuller, Wallace Brooks, and Marlin Tanck. Mr. Tanck deserves special recognition because he has contributed much in the way of criticism and constructive suggestions. In addition, he is the author of the exercise on fiscal policy in Chapter Four and of the description of how to write better essay examinations in Chapter Nine. The proofreading and suggestions offered by Dr. Burton Grover, J. B. Nelson, and my wife, Faith, were most helpful.

NORRIS M. SANDERS

Classroom Questions

ONE

❖

QUESTIONS DESIGNED FOR
MORE THAN MEMORY

Introduction

"THERE IS NOTHING NEW under the sun," states a verse in Ecclesiastes. This may be true, but old ideas can often be profitably viewed from new vantage points. The main topic of this book is as old as education, because questions and problems have long been used to motivate interest, to instruct, and to evaluate. However, even today the topic lends itself to further investigation. The basic hypotheses on which this book is built are these: First, teachers can lead students into all kinds of thinking through care-

1

ful use of questions, problems, and projects.[1] Second, some teachers intuitively ask questions of high quality, but far too many overemphasize those that require students only to remember, and practically no teachers make full use of all worthwhile kinds of questions. The objective of this book is to describe a practical plan to insure a varied intellectual atmosphere in a classroom. The approach is through a systematic consideration of questions that require students to *use* ideas, rather than simply to *remember* them.

Basic ideas underlying this study of questions come from the book *Taxonomy of Educational Objectives,* edited by B. S. Bloom, which presents an ingenious plan for classifying educational objectives.[2] Some explanation is necessary to show how a book on objectives has significance to the topic of questions. The authors of the *Taxonomy of Educational Objectives* were employed in writing college examinations and were troubled by the difficulty of composing tests that truly evaluated the success in attaining objectives set forth for various college subjects. Their purpose was to develop a system that could be used to classify any educational objective and thereby provide a useful pattern in a hopelessly confused area in educational thinking. They decided to concentrate their first book on the intellectual aspects of education and leave the emotional and physical for later study. Within this cognitive domain, they defined a number of categories of thinking that encompassed all intellectual objectives in education and named them "memory,"[3] "translation," "interpretation,"[4]

[1] To avoid the need for frequent repetition of certain terms, the word "question" shall be used to refer to any intellectual exercise calling for a response; this would include both problems and projects.

[2] Benjamin S. Bloom (ed.), *Taxonomy of Educational Objectives* (New York: Longmans, Green, 1956).

[3] In Bloom's book, the category of "memory" is called "knowledge." All categories, except this one, are given names of mental processes. The word "knowledge" is commonly used in education to refer to subject matter. "Memory" better describes the intellectual activity and is parallel with the names of the other categories.

[4] In Bloom's book, "translation," "interpretation," and "extrapolation" are all placed under the heading of "comprehension." "Transla-

"application," "analysis," "synthesis," and "evaluation." One of the ways they defined each category was by using examples of questions that required students to engage in the specified kind of thinking. This is the point at which the *Taxonomy of Educational Objectives* is carried in a new direction by the "taxonomy of questions" which is developed in this volume. The word "taxonomy" refers to a special system of classification in which the classes are sequential rather than arbitrary. The full meaning of the word will be clarified later in this chapter.

To follow the reasoning in this chapter, some *preliminary* definitions of Bloom's categories of thinking are required:

1. *Memory:* The student recalls or recognizes information.
2. *Translation:* The student changes information into a different symbolic form or language.
3. *Interpretation:* The student discovers relationships among facts, generalizations, definitions, values, and skills.
4. *Application:* The student solves a lifelike problem that requires the identification of the issue and the selection and use of appropriate generalizations and skills.
5. *Analysis:* The student solves a problem in the light of conscious knowledge of the parts and forms of thinking.
6. *Synthesis:* The student solves a problem that requires original, creative thinking.[5]
7. *Evaluation:* The student makes a judgment of good or bad, right or wrong, according to standards he designates.

Students can be led to think in each category through the use of such questions as these:

Memory: What is meant by "gerrymandering"? (The student is asked to recall the definition presented to him earlier.)

---

tion" and "interpretation" offer opportunities for distinct kinds of thinking and are treated as separate categories in this book; but "extrapolation" is not defined as a separate category.

[5] The reader is reminded that these preliminary definitions are by no means adequate for distinguishing the categories. They are submitted only as a necessary background to a discussion of the way in which ideas from the *Taxonomy of Educational Objectives* can be used by classroom teachers.

Translation: The *Encyclopaedia of the Social Sciences* defines "gerrymander" in this way:

Gerrymander is a term used to describe the abuse of power whereby the political party dominant at the time in a legislature arranges constituencies unequally so that its voting strength may count for as much as possible at elections and that of the other party or parties for as little as possible.

Restate this definition in your own words.

Interpretation: Each county in the diagram of the mythical state has about the same population and is dominated by the designated political party "A" or "B." The state must be divided into five voting districts of about equal population. Each district must contain three counties.

A	B	B	A	A
A	A	B	A	B
A	A	B	A	B

What is the greatest number of districts that Party A could control if it is in charge of the redistricting and chooses to gerrymander? What is the greatest number of districts that Party B could control if it is in charge of the redistricting and chooses to gerrymander? (The students have previously been given a definition of gerrymandering.)

Application: The mayor recently appointed a committee to study the fairness of the boundaries of the election districts in our community. Gather information about the present districts and the population in each. Determine whether the present city election districts are adequate. (The student is expected to apply principles of democracy studied in class to this new problem.)

Analysis: Analyze the reasoning in this quotation: "Human beings lack the ability to be fair when their own interests are involved. Party X controls the legislature and now it has taken upon itself the responsibility of redrawing the boundaries of the legislative election districts. We know in advance that our party will suffer."

Synthesis: (This question must follow the application question given above.) If current election districts in our community are inadequate, suggest how they might be redrawn.

Evaluation: Would you favor having your political party engage in gerrymandering if it had the opportunity?

Earlier it was suggested that memory questions excessively dominate education. This allegation can now be defined with greater precision. As a result of overusing the memory category, many teachers tend to offer students too few questions requiring translation, interpretation, application, analysis, synthesis, and evaluation.

Uses of the Taxonomy of Questions

A teacher who has mastered the taxonomy of questions can use it in a number of ways to improve the intellectual climate of his classroom. It offers a means for him to answer this question: "Am I offering all appropriate intellectual experiences in my classroom or am I overemphasizing some and neglecting others?" The answer can easily be found by classifying the questions asked on examinations, homework, and orally. Some teachers already do well in asking a variety of questions, but many will discover—as did this teacher—that memory questions play too large a part. The mastery of the characteristics of each category is a great help in writing better questions. As a teacher builds his units, he asks himself: What opportunities are there for application questions? What opportunities are there for synthesis questions?, etc. The teacher's knowledge of the format of each type of question helps him to be more sensitive to the opportunities for many kinds of thinking.

The taxonomy of questions provides a useful standard in evaluating instructional materials. Many textbooks offer only recall questions at the end of each chapter. More serious yet, the nature of the exposition in textbooks makes it difficult for teachers to write good questions of their own. Chapter Nine offers suggestions on ways to identify teaching materials that foster the use of a variety of questions.

Virtually every set of educational objectives mentions the goal of developing critical thinking. The problem is that there have been few satisfactory definitions of critical thinking; so the objective is frequently lost in the trip through instruction and evaluation. A precise and useful definition of the phrase is that it includes all thought processes beyond the memory category. A teacher who offers his students appropriate experiences in translation, interpretation, application, analysis, synthesis, and evaluation can be assured he is providing instruction in every intellectual aspect of critical thinking.

The taxonomy of questions suggests fruitful hypotheses for educational research, such as these:

1. Students who have more practice with intellectual skills will develop them to a greater degree than those who have less practice.
2. After a teacher studies the taxonomy, he is likely to offer his students a greater variety of intellectual experiences than he did before.
3. A greater emphasis on the teaching of the intellectual skills, other than the memory level, will not decrease the amount of knowledge the student retains.

"Learning by doing," an important idea in a prominent theory of learning, is given more precise meaning by the taxonomy of questions. A few years ago, most educators thought of learning as the process of filling a child's mind with knowledge in much the same manner that a pitcher is filled with water. This approach was unsatisfactory, partly because of the rapid rate of forgetting but more because of the tenuous relationship between knowledge and behavior. A student could know all about the Constitution of the United States and be able to recite a list of the obligations of citizenship without being a good citizen himself. At least partly as a result of these shortcomings, some educators devised a new concept of learning that viewed the student as an active participant in the process rather than a passive receptacle. The student was still expected to remember information, such as the characteristics of a good citizen; but, in addition, he was given an opportunity to live the role of a good citizen in the classroom. A problem arose when some teachers misinterpreted the new slogan "learn by doing" to mean that students must be engaged in activity with their hands and bodies in such projects as making dioramas, models, collages, and in acting out sociodramas. The taxonomy of questions helps to clarify "learning by doing" by demonstrating that a child can be sitting quietly at a desk and yet be vigorously engaged in any one of a number of kinds of mental activities.

Ideas Underlying the Taxonomy of Questions

Before developing full definitions and examples of all categories of questions, several ideas underlying the taxonomy must be clarified.

Bloom and his associates claim that any objective can be classified in their taxonomy and imply that any question can also be classified. However, experience shows that teachers working with the taxonomy of questions often disagree on the classification of a question and that all parties to the dispute can make good cases for their positions. Fortunately, this is not a severe handicap in the uses anticipated for the classroom teacher. The relationships between the categories of questions are similar to that between colors on a spectrum. There, the colors of red, orange, yellow, green, blue, indigo, and violet are plainly visible. Between each color, however, is an area that is neither one nor the other, but a part of both. The same seems true of the categories in the taxonomy. *The important point for teachers to remember is that difficulty in classifying any question is no detraction from the quality of the question.*

There are three factors entering into the determination of the kind of thinking that is brought about in the minds of students by any question. First, the nature of the question itself must be considered in terms of its classification in the taxonomy. A certain kind of question leads to a certain kind of thinking. Second, one must be aware of the knowledge of the subject that each student brings to the classroom. For example, suppose a teacher presents general differences between the beliefs of the Republican and Democratic parties and then asks students to study quotations from political speeches to determine which party's philosophy is best illustrated. A student who reads the newspaper with more than ordinary devotion might remember a quotation as being a part of a speech by a well-known member of one of the parties. For this student, the question on the quotation requires only memory, although he might corroborate his answer by interpretation. Other students who had not read the speech could reach the same answer legitimately by using only the category of interpretation.

The third factor that enters into the classification of a question concerns the instruction that precedes the asking of a question. In a civics course, one might ask: *Why might a congressman prefer a voice vote on a bill rather than a recorded vote of the "yeas" and "nays"?* If the answer was given in the text or by the teacher, then only memory is required from the student. However, students who are taught the role of a congressman should be able to infer the answer without being told. For the most part, teachers can anticipate the amount of knowledge students have on a subject and the mental processes they will use to arrive at an answer. There are exceptions, however, and it is wrong to assume that a question inevitably leads to a single category of thinking or that all students are necessarily using the same mental processes to arrive at an answer. Another example of the manner in which the thinking resulting from a question is influenced by the classroom context is illustrated in this example from American history: *Did the North or the South have the greater strength at the beginning of the Civil War?* Textbooks usually list the strengths of the North and the South, and then conclude that, although the South had certain advantages, the North had greater strength. To answer the question after reading the text requires only memory. However, the same question solicits more than memory if it is presented in a different way. Suppose the teacher assembles several pages of information concerning geography, industry, agriculture, transportation, military strength, and education of the North and the South in 1861. Some of the information would be germane to the problem and some purposely would not. Now the same question on the relative strength of the North and the South requires much more than memory. The student first determines the factors that are important in giving strength in a war fought at that time and then compares the strengths of the two sides.

Failure to recognize that instructional procedures enter into the kind of thinking required by a question leads to a common fallacy in education. Many educators advocate less emphasis on "what," "where," and "when" questions and more emphasis on "why" and "how" questions. The fallacy is the belief that a "why" or "how" question necessarily demands more than memory. The question: *Why did the United States enter a depression in 1929?* is only a memory question if the student is expected to give back the same neat little package of answers provided in the text or in the teacher's lecture. "Why" and "how" questions are excellent when they are presented in a way that leads students to figure out the answers—not simply to remember them.

The authors of the *Taxonomy of Educational Objectives* state that their categories are sequential and cumulative. In other words, each category of thinking has unique elements but also includes some form of all lower categories. The following chart illustrates this idea:

```
                                                      EVALUA-
                                                       TION
                                                        ↑
                                        SYNTHESIS   Synthesis
                                            ↑           ↑
                            ANALYSIS    Analysis    Analysis
                                ↑           ↑           ↑
                APPLICA-    Applica-    Applica-    Applica-
                  TION        tion        tion        tion
                    ↑           ↑           ↑           ↑
   INTERPRE-    Interpre-   Interpre-   Interpre-   Interpre-
     TATION       tation      tation      tation      tation
        ↑           ↑           ↑           ↑           ↑
   TRANS-      Transla-    Transla-    Transla-    Transla-    Transla-
   LATION        tion        tion        tion        tion        tion
      ↑           ↑           ↑           ↑           ↑           ↑
MEMORY  Memory  Memory    Memory      Memory      Memory      Memory
```

A question should be classified at its highest level. Evaluation stands at the top of the ladder and includes all lower kinds of thought plus that which is solely evaluation.[6] The chart also illustrates that attention to higher categories of thinking does not imply a neglect of memory, because memory is the only thought process that is a part of every kind of thinking.

There are both simple and complex questions within each category. For example, the memory level includes questions soliciting a single fact: *Who was the first President of the United States?* At the other end of the memory scale is this question: *Trace the evolution of United States tariff policy from 1789 to the present.* The implication is that all teachers from the primary grades through graduate school will find it possible to use every one of the categories in their classes. The differences in the questions offered at various grade levels should be in the *complexity* of the thinking, rather than in the *kind* of thinking.

The same point applies in teaching the slow and rapid learners. A superficial appraisal of the levels of questions might lead to

---

[6] The word "taxonomy" comes from science and refers to this form of a sequential and cumulative system of classification.

the conclusion that slow learners should restrict their efforts to the memory category, while the bright children should be permitted to range through all levels. This is an error, because there are simple questions in each category of thinking. The slow learners often find education frustrating and lacking in interest; these children, above all, need variety in their educational diet. Experimentation may show that students who have difficulty with memory questions will have greater success with those that provide all necessary facts and ask the students to use them.

Finally, one must remember that the words used as names of the categories have stipulated definitions that depart somewhat from common usage. Teachers who are communicating about questions must specify when they are using the specialized meaning.

Placing the Taxonomy in Perspective

During the last few years, it has become fashionable to emphasize intellectual processes and subject matter in education. The taxonomy of questions fits into this trend. There is little doubt that humans exhibit rational behavior, but some irrationality is equally apparent in man. Teachers who concern themselves with the possible uses of the taxonomy of questions must not lose sight of the fact that concern for the quality of thought in the classroom is inadequate as a total philosophy of education. Psychologists have proven that emotional atmosphere in the classroom has a great deal to do with any learning that might result. The receptivity of students for any kind of classroom learning is conditioned by both in-school and out-of-school experiences. Educators took a great step forward when they discovered that they must be concerned with the whole child—not simply with his mind.

* * *

Each of the next seven chapters defines and illustrates a category. All sample questions are from the field of social studies, but the definitions apply equally well to other academic disciplines.

Specialists in other subjects are encouraged to apply the taxonomy to their areas. The final chapters contain suggestions for writing questions. The words of caution throughout the book regarding possible misinterpretation and misuse of the taxonomy worth serious consideration.

QUESTIONS ON CHAPTER ONE

A book advocating the imaginative use of questions to promote learning must certainly practice what it preaches. One reason for offering questions at the end of each chapter is to aid the reader in a self-evaluation of his understanding of the taxonomy of questions. However, there is more than this involved. Some questions are designed to focus attention on ideas most worthy of remembering, and others are intended to deepen or extend the understanding of these ideas. For example, a chapter might describe the characteristics of a form of question; the reader may then be asked to compose questions that exhibit the characteristics.

The following questions are not written to stump the reader; hopefully, he will get all of them correct. The proponents of programmed learning stress the idea that knowledge is reinforced if the learner answers the question correctly and then is immediately informed that his answer is correct. Thus, the answers to the questions are included at the end of each chapter.

1._____ True or False: The taxonomy of questions is based on the idea that a student can often be led to engage in a certain kind of thinking by presenting him a certain kind of question.

2._____ According to a hypothesis of this book, which one of the seven categories of thought is often overemphasized by teachers? (A) memory; (B) translation; (C) interpretation; (D) application; (E) analysis; (F) synthesis; (G) evaluation.

3._____ The taxonomy of questions deals mainly with which of the following? (A) intellectual learning; (B) emotional learning; (C) physical learning; (D) none of the above.

4.____ True or False: The word "question" is defined in this book to include only interrogative statements.

5.____ True or False: The taxonomy of questions has significance for classroom evaluation but not for instruction.

6. What might a teacher do to determine whether he is offering his students opportunities for a variety of thought? (Write an answer in two or three sentences.)

7. What is the relationship between the taxonomy of questions and critical thinking? (Write an answer in two or three sentences.)

8.____ True or False: The taxonomy of questions was formulated with the idea that every question should be subject to classification in a single category. This goal has been largely but not completely achieved. On some questions a case can be made for classifying a question in each of several categories.

9.____ True or False: A question that cannot be classified with certainty into a category is a faulty question for use in the classroom.

10. Check all factors that enter into determining the classification of a question into a certain category of the taxonomy:

   ____A. The kind of thinking anticipated to arrive at an answer

   ____B. The previous knowledge of a student on the subject of the question

   ____C. The instruction on the topic of the question that precedes the asking of the question

   ____D. The use of the question for evaluation rather than instruction

   ____E. The subject field in which the question is asked

11.____ True or False: It is possible for a question that starts with the word "why" to require a student only to remember.

12.____ True or False: A question presented to a class may be correctly answered by two students who use different categories of thinking to arrive at their answers.

13.____ True or False: The more accurately a teacher knows the amount of knowledge that students have on a subject, the more accurately the teacher can predict the category of thinking brought about by questions on the subject.

14._____ True or False: Through different patterns of instruction, a teacher can lead students to answer the following question by either memory alone or by more than memory: "What were the causes of World War I?"

15._____ True or False: There is no logical order to the categories of questions.

16._____ True or False: In theory an application question always includes interpretive thinking.

17._____ How many categories of thought are not included in the analysis category? (The answer is a number.)

18._____ In what category would a question be classified that requires interpretation, translation, and memory?

19._____ True or False: A good way to learn the meaning of the categories of questions is to consult the dictionary.

20._____ True or False: A general principle in the taxonomy of questions is that the higher on the list a question is classified, the more difficult the question is to answer.

21. On the basis of the ideas developed in Chapter One, which of the following questions would require only memory and which would require more than memory? (Remember that you are *not* to answer true or false.)

_____A. T. or F: The taxonomy of questions deals with intellectual education.

_____B. T. or F: The most important use of the taxonomy of questions is to provide the rationale for classroom research.

_____C. Write a question based on the information in Chapter One that requires more than memory.

_____D. T. or F: A list of provocative questions would often be a useful part of a lesson plan.

_____E. T. or F: One value in practicing the classification of questions by teachers is that it helps teachers to learn the classifications.

_____F. T. or F: It is always better to ask a question above the memory level than a question that is only at the memory level.

22. Three citizenship teachers taught the concept of "conflict of interest" in the following ways:

Teacher I wrote the definition of conflict of interest on the board and presented six examples of the operation of the concept to the students. After erasing the definition from the board, the teacher asked several members of the class to repeat it orally. A few days later the students were asked on a test to define conflict of interest and write two examples.

Teacher II wrote a definition of conflict of interest on the board. He had collected six examples and told two of them to the class to clarify the meaning of the concept. After erasing the definition from the board, the teacher asked the students to repeat it. He then gave students practice in recognizing the operation of conflict of interest by describing situations in which a person had to make a decision and asking the students to determine whether or not there was a conflict of interest involved. In this part of the instruction he used two more of his examples. The last two examples were used on a test in which the students decided which of a number of cases illustrated conflict of interest.

Teacher III did not give students a definition of conflict of interest. He said that the meaning of the phrase could be determined from three examples of the operation of the concept which he presented. After giving some time for studying the examples and composing the definitions, the teacher asked that some be read to the class. The one chosen by the class as the best was assigned to be remembered. The assignment for the following day was to find examples of the operation of conflict of interest in the newspaper or to make up plausible examples. Later, on a test the students were asked to write a definition of conflict of interest and to make up a new situation illustrating the idea.

_____A. Which teacher taught the concept of interest wholly on the memory level?

_____B. Which teacher had the students spend most time on learning and evaluating the concept?

_____C. Which teacher taught the concept in a manner in which a student might answer the questions correctly but not really understand the meaning of the phrase?

_____D. Some educators believe that students have better understanding of an idea and remember it longer if they take part in its formulation. Which of the three teachers would most likely accept this belief?

23.＿＿＿ Which one of the following reasons is the best explanation why Teacher II did not use all his examples of conflict of interest in the initial instruction? (A) Not all his examples were good ones. (B) He was trying to save time. (C) He was saving some examples necessary to give students evaluation questions in which they would be called upon to recognize the idea of the conflict of interest in a new setting. (D) He believed that the students could form their own definitions of conflict of interest.

24. Which teacher in Question 22 do you believe used the most appropriate procedures for instructing and evaluating the concept of conflict of interest? (Tell why in a paragraph.)

ANSWERS TO QUESTIONS ON
CHAPTER ONE

1. True. The reason the word "often" is used in the question is that sometimes the student arrives at an answer by a line of thinking the teacher does not anticipate.
2. A.
3. A.
4. False. The definition of "question" is stipulated to include any problem or project as well as interrogative statements.
5. False. The questions in the taxonomy are to be applied to problems of motivation and instruction, as well as to evaluation.
6. A teacher can classify questions that he uses in instruction and evaluation to determine whether he is leading his students to all appropriate kinds of thinking.
7. The thought processes used in the categories above memory serve as a useful definition of the cognitive aspects of critical thinking.
8. True.
9. False. The question may be either good or poor, but this distinction is not determined by its ease of classification.
10. A, B, and C should be checked.
11. True. When the student has been told "why" before answering the questions, he can answer from memory. If the student must figure out "why," the classification is above memory.

12. True. One may remember the answer while another may deduce it.

13. True.

14. True. The teacher can structure the instruction so that students are required only to remember the causes or so that they have a part in figuring out some causes on the basis of evidence presented to them.

15. False. The categories are in a logical order from memory to evaluation. However, later chapters will point to some weaknesses in the logic.

16. True. Every category theoretically includes all kinds of thinking listed below it; so application includes translation and memory and the kind of thinking that is uniquely application.

17. Two. Synthesis and evaluation are listed above analysis and are not included in it.

18. Interpretation. A question is always classified at the highest level of thinking it produces. Interpretation is highest of the three.

19. False. The definitions of the categories unfortunately do not correspond to the common dictionary meanings of the words.

20. False. There are easy and difficult questions possible in every category. Evaluation stands at the top of the ladder, but an evaluation question can be simple. A memory question can be easy or difficult.

21. A. memory; B. more than memory; C. more than memory; D. more than memory; E. more than memory; F. more than memory. In all questions, except A, the student must make a simple judgment or deduction. For example, in B, the chapter mentioned the use of the taxonomy as offering fruitful hypotheses for research, but it did not suggest that the research use was more important than any other use. (A weakness of this question is that the answer depends on the ability of the reader to remember ideas stated in the chapter and to distinguish them from simple deductions made by the reader. The question is included to encourage teachers to form the habit of making this distinction between questions requiring memory and those leading to more than memory.)

22. A. I; B. III; C. I; D. III.

23. C.

24. This judgment of the most appropriate instructional proce-

dure is the kind of problem that will later be identified in the evaluation category. One characteristic of evaluation is that the answer is at least partly subjective. In my judgment Teacher II used the most appropriate means of instructing the concept. The idea of conflict of interest is complicated enough, so that a student might be able to recite a definition without being able to apply the meaning to new situations. On the other hand, the idea of conflict of interest is not important enough to take time for inducing the definition from examples. The process used by Teacher III does not appear to give any more insight into the concept than the procedure used by Teacher II. However, there are occasions in education when Teacher III's approach would be the best.

TWO

❖

MEMORY

Emphasizing the Important

THE MEMORY CATEGORY requires the student to recognize or recall information. A question is framed in such a way that if the student remembers information presented to him he will know it applies to the question. The student is not asked to compare or relate or make any inductive or deductive leap *on his own*. If a textbook contains a section comparing British, French, and Spanish colonial policies, and a student is asked to make the same comparison, he has only to remember and the question falls in the memory category.

The greatest problem in this category is not how to write good test items but rather how to determine the knowledge that is worth remembering and how to structure learning so that the emphasis is really on the knowledge judged most important. There appears to be a general overemphasis on trivial information in the social studies. The easiest questions to compose ask the student to remember specific information. What questions would a teacher most likely ask of fourth-graders who read the following paragraph from a unit on the Navaho Indians?

After the sheep were safely in the corral, Joe started for the *hogan*. That is what the Navahos call their houses. The hogan was nearly round. Its walls were made of logs, with mud plaster in the cracks. The roof of the hogan was made of logs covered with earth.[1]

The obvious questions are these:

1. What do the Navaho Indians call their houses?
2. What shape are the Navaho houses?
3. With what material do the Navahos make their houses?

The teacher scans the textbook to find facts and then asks the students to remember them. This procedure leads to emphasizing the inconsequential, rather than the substantial.

One of the first steps in developing a unit is to determine the knowledge that is most important and therefore deserves the most attention. This process is facilitated by speculating on some ideas in regard to facts, definitions, generalizations, values, and skills.

Facts

The narrowest definition of "fact" stresses knowledge that comes from direct observation. A scientist gathers this knowledge, often with the aid of measuring instruments. "Fact" as defined in this manner allows for little or no interpretation. A broader use

[1] Herbert H. Gross *et al.*, *Exploring Near and Far* (Chicago: Follett, 1959), p. 73.

of the word emphasizes that a fact is noncontroversial. An interpretation that goes beyond direct observation is still called fact provided it is not subject to much disagreement. The depression of 1929 was not directly observable even though many of its manifestations could be seen. However, there is little question that there was a depression in the United States starting in 1929. In this sense it is a fact.

Specific factual information serves three roles in education. First, some facts are important in themselves. For example, every citizen should know his legal rights when arrested. Second, some facts are worth remembering because a cultured person is expected to possess them. Ashley Montagu wrote a book entitled *The Cultured Man* in which he identified a vast quantity of information he believed an educated person should possess.[2] We might disagree with his selection, but most would agree that there is a body of factual information not likely to be useful in a practical sense but which students should be taught and expected to remember. The proper boundaries of this knowledge are subject to disagreement. The third and most important role of facts is the providing of building blocks for generalizations, laws, and principles. For the most part, facts should serve as a means to an end rather than as ends in themselves. When a teacher approaches a new unit, he should ask himself: "What are the most important generalizations that deserve to be emphasized? What facts are necessary to develop these generalizations?"

Definitions, Generalizations, and Values

Definitions are the designated meanings of words. A definition is not a fact because the relationship between the word and the entity to which it refers is arbitrarily assigned by man. William Shakespeare spoke truly when he wrote, "That which we call a

[2] Ashley Montagu, *The Cultured Man* (Cleveland: World Publishing Co., 1958).

rose by any other name would smell as sweet." In any unit of study there are likely to be words that are new to the student. Some are more important than others as is illustrated in the following list suggested for consideration in a sixth-grade unit on Greece: Acropolis, agora, allies, Athena, citizen, colonies, constitution, democracy, Golden Age, Parthenon, peninsula, and terraces.[3] Certainly the meanings of words such as "citizen," "constitution," and "democracy" deserve more attention than "terrace" or even "agora" and "Athena." The latter have significance in the unit on Greece but are not likely to enter into study in subsequent history.

A generalization is a statement that declares the common characteristics of a group of ideas or things. Important and widely accepted generalizations are often called principles or laws; but most are not graced with such a title. Scholars constantly seek to discover generalizations that make life more understandable and learning more economical. For example, a historian who specializes in the political history in Europe from 1500 to 1789 might generalize that the common pattern of government featured:

1. Absolute monarchy based on the "divine right of kings"
2. A privileged noble class
3. Restricted civil liberties
4. An established church

Students can learn the meaning of these generalizations and know much about the government of this period without duplicating the prolonged study of the historian. Of course the historian has a much deeper comprehension of the subject, but the generalizations make it possible for students to get a reasonably accurate understanding within a short period.

The superior teacher chooses generalizations on the basis of his study and knowledge of his subject. In some schools, the curriculum bulletins specify the main generalizations to be taught.

[3] O. Stuart Hamer et al., Exploring the Old World (Chicago: Follett, 1960), p. 86.

Teachers who follow the lead of a textbook have the generalizations selected for them by the author. To illustrate the process of identifying generalizations, the following examples are taken from a fourth-grade textbook unit on people who live in a desert-grazing culture.[4] The book is organized by type-regions; so the assumption is that other desert-grazing cultures are similar to the ones described in southeast United States and in North Africa. The text is written as a story of Joe Manygoats, the young Navaho Indian, and Ali the Arab. These generalizations are implicit in the story, rather than stated directly:

1. Lack of rain causes deserts to be sparse in vegetation.
2. Life in the desert is difficult.
   A. The home is crude and the family moves frequently.
   B. Medical help is not available.
   C. Life is close to nature and welfare often dependent on the caprice of nature.
   D. Transportation is by foot or animal.
3. People of the desert know little about the outside world.
4. Children play an important economic function in the family at an early age.
5. Desert people are largely self-sufficient.
6. Desert people often are happy in spite of their hardships.
7. Ethical and vocational education are family functions in the desert.
8. Economic exchange takes the form of barter.
9. Population density is low on the desert for economic reasons.
10. Communication of news on the desert is by word of mouth.
11. Natural resources can be destroyed by improper use.
12. The people who live on the desert are concerned about religion and often interpret their problems in religious terms.

The type-region organization in story form makes interesting reading but raises a danger that the students will miss the generalizations or will overgeneralize.

[4] Gross, *op. cit.*, pp. 66–106.

A value differs from a generalization in that it expresses a judgment of quality. It states that something is good or bad; fair or unfair; beautiful or ugly; right or wrong; useful or useless; important or trivial; true or false. The Ten Commandments and the Beatitudes are examples of values against which behavior can be judged. In a number of nations, including the United States, democracy is one of the prime values. The concept is defined as respect for the individual, the rule of the majority with concern for the minority, and the use of reason and discussion to settle differences. These standards are useful in judging the quality of developments in the stream of history.

Values must be treated carefully in the schools because of disagreement on their nature and source. The book that is great literature to one critic is obscene to another. The arguments as to whether certain values are absolute or relative are not likely to be settled soon. In spite of these problems, it is imperative that students learn to evaluate, because life demands evaluation. One of the highest categories in the taxonomy of questions deals with this form of thinking, but the subject of values is also pertinent to the memory category. Before values can be used, they must be in the minds of students on the recall level. In addition, it is not enough to study the values of our own culture, because part of the meaning of these values is apparent only through comparison with competing systems.

Statements of values are not found in textbooks nearly as often as are value judgments. A value judgment is the use of a value in determining the quality of an idea. A textbook may state: "Socrates was a great man." The value implied is that intellectual curiosity and humility are prized character traits. The value judgment is that Socrates measured up favorably to these traits and therefore was great.

Attention to definitions, generalizations and values is vitally important in framing good questions, for four reasons. First, this form of knowledge is generally the most important—the most worthy of learning. Second, teachers will find it much easier to compose questions that require a variety of intellectual activities if they concentrate on generalizations and values. Third, educational research indicates that widely applied generalizations and values are less likely to be forgotten than most other forms of knowledge. Fourth, educational psychologists who have studied the "transfer of training" conclude that the best way to prepare students for an unknown future is to instruct them in the use of generalizations and values that are likely to have fruitful application.

Skills

One of the best ways to define skills is by listing their characteristics:

1. A skill is a physical, emotional, and/or intellectual process.
2. A skill requires knowledge, but knowledge alone does not insure proficiency.
3. A skill can be used in a variety of situations.
4. A skill can be improved through practice.
5. A skill is often made up of a number of subskills that can be identified and practiced separately.

We too often ask our students to *use* a skill without adequate information on its nature. Suppose a teacher is providing instruction in the skill of judging the reliability of reports in the news. After reading several descriptions of an event that is subject to controversy, such as a race riot, the teacher might ask, "Which report of this incident is most reliable?" Before the students undertake to answer such a question, they should have instruction in the skill identified by Robert Ennis as "judging whether an observation statement is reliable."

1. Observation statements tend to be more reliable if the observer
   A. Was unemotional, alert and disinterested.
   B. Was skilled at observing the sort of thing observed.
   C. Had sensory equipment that was in good condition.

    D. Has a reputation for veracity.

    E. Used precise techniques.

    F. Had no preconception about the way the observation would turn out.

2. Observation statements tend to be more reliable if the observation conditions

    A. Were such that the observer had good access.

    B. Provided a satisfactory medium of observation.

3. Observation statements tend to be more reliable to the extent that the statement

    A. Is close to being a statement of direct observation.

    B. Is corroborated.

    C. Is corroboratable.

4. Observation statements, if based on a record, tend to be more reliable if the record

    A. Was made at the time of observation.

    B. Was made by the person making the statement.

    C. Is believed by the person making the statement to be correct—either because he so believed at the time the record was made, or because he believes it was the record-maker's habit to make correct records.

5. Observation statements tend to be more reliable than inferences made from them.[5]

The first instruction of this skill should be made on the memory level. After studying the definition of the skill, the students could be asked questions, such as these:

1. What are the characteristics of the observer of an event that would give you greater confidence in the accuracy of his observation?

2. What conditions at the scene of an event promote accuracy on the part of an observer?

3. What type of records of an event are most reliable?

Students who possess this information are ready to make a reasoned judgment of the relative reliability of several conflicting reported observations of the race riot.

[5] Robert Ennis, "A Concept of Critical Thinking," *Harvard Educational Review*, Winter, 1962, pp. 81–111.

Some skills used in the social studies receive proper emphasis, but others are neglected. Most social studies textbooks in the intermediate grades do a splendid job in providing information on the nature and use of maps and globes. Two other skills that are often well taught concern the use of charts and graphs and the use of the library to find information. However, there is a general deficiency in consideration of the type of thinking skills identified in the following list composed by the Committee of Examiners for the Test of Developed Ability in the Social Studies:

1. Arrive at or identify warranted conclusions
2. Draw or recognize valid inferences
3. Distinguish fact from opinion
4. Separate relevant from irrelevant information
5. Form or identify generalizations
6. Compare and contrast points-of-view
7. Formulate or identify basic assumptions and premises
8. Marshal or identify main points or central issues
9. Reconstruct or identify attitudes, outlooks, motivations or bias
10. Supply or identify data or appropriate information necessary to support or refute conclusions or generalizations
11. Assess the sufficiency of data to support given conclusions
12. Arrive at some kind of synthesis so as to produce a reasoned judgment

Another fine list of intellectual skills is to be found in the article by Robert Ennis.[6]

The memory category is indispensable on all levels of thinking. The more important and useful knowledge a student possesses, the better his chances for success in other categories of thought. However, the importance of the memory category should not be permitted to completely overshadow its three weaknesses. The first is the inevitably rapid rate of forgetting. Numerous studies show that arbitrary facts are forgotten more quickly than generalizations or principles and even the latter have limited

[6] Ennis, *op. cit.*, pp. 81–111.

longevity.[7] Teachers frequently take an unrealistic attitude toward forgetting. If a student in a study hall asks a social studies teacher to help him with an algebra problem or the diagramming of a sentence, the teacher isn't embarrassed to say that he cannot remember the first thing about either subject. But the same social studies teacher is aghast when students do not remember his subject. Retention of knowledge is too ephemeral to serve as the goal of education. Lists of objectives always go further than the remembrance of knowledge, but in practice many teachers make memory their sole objective.

The second weakness is that memorized knowledge does not necessarily represent a high level of understanding. A student who memorizes the Preamble to the United States Constitution and records it accurately on an examination may possess only a vague or distorted idea of its meaning.

The third weakness of an education concentrating on memory is that it neglects other intellectual processes learned only through practice. A student best learns to draw inductive conclusions by practice—not by memorizing the inductive conclusions of others. A student best learns to organize ideas by performing the process of organizing, rather than by memorizing an orderly pattern of ideas. The following chapters describe other mental activities that students should be encouraged to practice.

QUESTIONS ON CHAPTER TWO

1._____ True or False: A memory question asks students to recognize or recall information presented to them earlier.
2._____ True or False: An essay question could be in the memory category.

[7] Alfred Dietze and George Jones gave high-school students a four-page pamphlet on Arkwright to read. In a test given immediately afterward, the students retained an average of 54.6 percent, but one hundred days later they remembered only 23.4 percent. Jones found that college students retained an average of 62 percent from a lecture in immediate recall but only 24 percent after eight weeks. As described in Ernest Horn, *Methods of Instruction in the Social Studies* (New York: Scribner's, 1937), p. 488.

3. Write two or three of the most obvious questions based on the following paragraph from a sixth-grade social studies book:
"In 594 B.C. Solon came into power in Athens. Although a noble, he understood the problems of poor farmers and of common people. He set free those who had been sold into slavery to pay their debts. Of course, this action did not free all slaves in Greece."[8]

4. Classify the questions you wrote for the previous question as "memory" or "more than memory."

5. In each of the four parts of this question place a check before the letter of the statement that you believe presents the more important knowledge for development in a junior high school world geography course. Check one generalization, one fact, one definition, and one value judgment.[9]

Definitions:

_____A. Socialism is "a system under which the government owns and operates farms, factories, mines, and other means of production."

_____B. A samovar is an urn used for heating water.

Facts:

_____A. Leningrad has 2,888,000 people.

_____B. In October, 1957, the Russians launched the first satellite, Sputnik I.

Generalizations:

_____A. Today Soviet leaders are working unceasingly for world revolution.

_____B. Nearly all of the houses have small front porches.

Value Judgments:

_____A. We are glad that in the United States we can own our own homes and farms and that we can work for ourselves.

_____B. "I've never seen such big cabbages," Frank said admiringly.

6._____ True or False: Any generalization found in a unit will be more important than any fact found in the unit.

---

[8] Hamer, *op. cit.*, p. 94.
[9] All statements in this question are quoted from a unit on Soviet Lands in the textbook: Prudence Cutright and John Jarolimek (eds.), *Living As World Neighbors* (New York: Macmillan, 1962).

7._____ True or False: Generalizations *tend* to be more important than facts.

8._____ Which is *not* a weakness of memory questions? (A) Memory is unnecessary in the higher categories of thought. (B) The ability to remember an idea does not necessarily indicate a deep understanding of the idea. (C) Memorized ideas are subject to rapid forgetting. (D) Preoccupation with memory questions prevents practice of other kinds of thinking.

9._____ True or False: The first instruction of a skill should be on the memory level.

RELATING THE TAXONOMY OF QUESTIONS TO A UNIT
OF YOUR CHOICE

The reader has now tasted the kind of short-answer questions that are presented at the end of each chapter to review, reinforce, and provide simple practice in the use of the main ideas. In this chapter and subsequent ones, questions are offered asking the reader to relate the ideas to a unit he chooses. The object is not so much to develop a unit as it is to give practice in writing questions in each category. One may prefer to read all chapters before writing his own questions.

10. This chapter emphasizes the need to distinguish between important and less important ideas and offers factors that enter into this decision. Draw these factors together, with others you believe to be pertinent, into a list of considerations that would be helpful in separating the wheat from the chaff in a unit.

11. Select a unit you wish to develop along the lines suggested in this volume. Choose a topic that you know most about, because this makes imaginative questioning easier. Using the ideas assembled in the previous problem, make a list of subject matter and skills deserving main attention in your unit. After listing these, review your choices to see whether you have included definitions, generalizations, values, and skills. If any of these forms of knowledge is missing, reconsider to satisfy yourself that it should not be included.

ANSWERS TO QUESTIONS ON
CHAPTER TWO

1. True.
2. True.
3. Some obvious questions are these:
   a. Who was Solon?
   b. When did Solon come to power in Athens?
   c. Did Solon understand the problems of the poor farmer?
   d. What happened to people in Athens who did not pay their debts?
   e. True or False: After the time of Solon there were no more slaves in Athens.
4. The questions listed are in the memory category and several are of doubtful importance. Perhaps the reader was more successful in composing a greater variety.
5. In all cases one statement is obviously more important than the other. The point of the question is to illustrate the wide range of significance of ideas in a single chapter.
6. False.
7. True.
8. A.
9. True.

THREE

❖

TRANSLATION

Definition of Translation

AN IDEA can be expressed in several different forms of communication, such as oral, written, pictorial, or graphic. Some examples are pictures, graphs, charts, maps, models, sociodramas, poems, outlines, summaries, detailed statements, statements in technical language, and statements in layman's language. Translation is the intellectual process of changing ideas in a communication into parallel forms.

Translation thinking is quite literal and does not require students to discover intricate relationships, implications, or subtle meanings. The student identifies one part of the original communication at a time and translates it into the new form. For example, suppose this problem is presented: *Tell the meaning of the following sentence from the Declaration of Independence in your own words:*

We hold these truths to be self-evident, that all men are created equal, that they are endowed by their creator with certain inalienable rights, that among these are life, liberty and the pursuit of happiness.

A translated answer might be: "We believe it is obvious that no humans are born with any special advantages. God gives everyone rights that cannot be given away, including the right to live in freedom and to seek contentment." The student translates sentence by sentence and phrase by phrase. This answer does not show full understanding of the quotation. It does show that the student knows the general meaning of the words at a higher level than is required by rote memorization of the passage.

There is always some skill involved in changing a communication to a parallel form, but translation questions do not emphasize this aspect. For example, if students are asked to draw a picture representing ideas expressed in a communication, the teacher is not so concerned with the quality of the art as with the accuracy of the portrayal of the ideas. A student who has no particular art talent is not at a disadvantage. If the translation requires making an outline, the teacher is more concerned with the selection of ideas that with the mechanics of outlining. This is an arbitrary part of the definition of translation and is included only to distinguish it from higher levels of thinking. Questions are assigned to higher categories than translation if they stress the use of a definition, generalization, value, or skill.

Examples of Translation

Questions calling for translation are relatively easy to compose. Following are examples:

1. This classic translation question is frequently used. When a student answers a question by parroting the words of the text,

the teacher asks for translation: "Now answer the question in your own words." In effect, this means: Translate the ideas from one communication (the textbook) to another (the student's own language).

2. In the lower elementary grades, one of the common forms of translation is from words to pictures or vice versa. Normally, textbooks on this level are well illustrated. When the text describes the operation of a coal mine and shows a cross section of it, the teacher can ask students to put their fingers on the place where the men will mine the coal or to point to the miner's safety helmet. In evaluating the unit, the teacher can use the opaque projector to show a different picture of a cross section of a mine that shows the *same* kind of situation. Capital letters could be printed at various points on the new picture and students asked to copy the letter that is on the miner's safety helmet or the letter on the coal that the men will mine next.

The same form of question can be used with more mature students. The "devil theory" in foreign relations is the false belief that if the major threat to our nation were removed, everything would be rosy. In other words, if communism were vanquished, the United States would live in an untroubled world community. Several years ago, the *Detroit News* published a cartoon quite close to a presentation of the "devil theory." If the cartoon is to be used to evaluate knowledge of the concept on the final examination, it should not be used in the original instruction. The question on the examination might be: *What idea that we studied in this unit is close to the main point the artist makes in this cartoon?*

3. A variation of the use of pictures in translation requires the student to compose a picture. This is illustrated in the following problem on "the revolution of rising expectations." After studying various manifestations of this idea, students are assigned thus: *Draw a poster depicting the meaning of the revolution of rising expectations. The main emphasis should be on translation of the idea, rather than on the art work. Those who are not talented in*

AND, BELOW THE SURFACE . . . ?

COMMUNIST ANTI-U-S- AGITATION

U.S.-FOREIGN POLICY

FAR-EAST EMERGING NATIONALISMS

DESIRE FOR HIGHER LIVING STANDARDS

FEAR OF INVOLVEMENT IN NUCLEAR WAR

TRADITIONAL ANTI-IMPERIALISM

art may use stick figures or describe in detail a picture that would represent the idea. One pupil drew negroid and mongolian-type people in primitive dress running up a stairway. At the bottom were crude huts and the words "poverty," "ignorance," and "disease." The steps were labeled with problems of newly independent people, such as "loss of assistance from the mother country," "economic turmoil," "civil war," and "cold war involvement." At the top were symbols of material progress. Such a picture demonstrates an insight into this concept on the translation level because all the ideas were presented to the student in oral or written form and he had only to represent them in a picture.

4. When students at any grade level are asked to read a selection that is a little more difficult than some of them can handle, a

good type of question asks them to match paraphrased sentences or paragraphs. The teacher rewrites the difficult sentences or paragraphs into simpler language and asks students to find the sentences or paragraphs in the reading that say the same things. For example, a generalization is made in the following sentence: "In 1787 a bicameral legislature was in existence in every state except Pennsylvania."[1] A teacher could rewrite the sentence to read: "At the time of the writing of the United States Constitution all states, except one, had legislatures made up of two houses." A student who recognizes that the two sentences say approximately the same thing understands the meaning of bicameral legislature. A series of questions of this nature make a good assignment and are easily corrected. Notice that this type of question asks students to recognize translation, rather than to translate. This, of course, is less demanding but is justified when the teacher wishes to keep the exercise in objective-question form or when he suspects that the ideas may be too difficult for the student to translate.

Another form of translation question places greater burden on the students by having them paraphrase sentences that contain important ideas without repeating more than one or two of the main nouns, verbs, or adjectives.

5. The translation of ideas into a sociodrama occasionally serves as an excellent learning exercise. Students are asked to act out an episode based on study of a situation. Nobody learns lines, but each simply plays a part. One junior high-school history teacher assigns such problems as these to a committee of students: (A) *Plan and present a sociodrama showing the impressment of seamen by the English during the Jefferson administration. (B) Plan and present a sociodrama of a cabinet meeting during Washington's administration. Be sure to bring out the differences in thinking between Hamilton and Jefferson.*

A sociodrama can be more structured. In a "special help" class

---

[1] Philip Dorf, *Visualized American Government* (New York: Oxford Book Co., 1961), p. 41.

on the secondary level, the following procedure worked well: In the study of how a bill becomes a law on the national level in the United States, the class acted out the legislative process. First, the class studied the textbook on the subject. Next, each student was assigned a role; some were members of the House of Representatives and others of the Senate. Each member of Congress was assigned to several committees. The members of Congress were divided among Democrats and Republicans in the same proportion as in the current national legislature. Students also played the part of the President, members of the Supreme Court, and John Q. Public. The teacher guided the thinking by a series of problems, such as these: "A farm bill is to be introduced in Congress. All people who believe they have the right to introduce this bill raise their hands." The text had said that any member of the Senate or House of Representatives could introduce the bill. The translation requires students to relate this idea to their role in the sociodrama. "If the bill is introduced first in the House of Representatives which of you will be the first to study the wisdom and necessity of this bill after the first reading?" The text had described the committee system and named the various committees.

John Q. Public was assigned to enter the legislative process at appropriate points. For instance, when the bill reached committee hearing in the House, he communicated with appropriate committee members via letter, telegram, and personal visits. The emphasis was on the legislative process and no effort was made to define the farm bill or to discuss it. The questions generally asked students to determine the next possible step in the process of making a law. Questions in this exercise are essentially translation, because students first studied the process in the text or in some other communication and then translated the *same* ideas into a sociodrama. In practice, a teacher probably would not restrict himself to translation questions. For example, when a bill is in a committee, the teacher might raise the question of the wisdom of having seniority determine the chairmanship. Provided this had not been previously explored by the teacher or the text, students would be engaged in a category of thinking to be identified later as evaluation.

In concluding this chapter, a word of caution is in order. The mechanics of translating an idea from one medium to another must not be permitted to be out of proportion to the importance of the idea. This frequently happens when students are asked to construct a model or to perform some elaborate drama. It is not necessary to build a guillotine in order to understand the part it played in the French Revolution. The sociodrama on the legislative process took three class periods to plan and execute. This amount of time seems justified because of the importance of the subject, while the same amount of time devoted to a Hawaiian luau would be questionable. Curriculum bulletins often list many activities of this nature which are time-consuming and not necessary to accomplish the defined objectives. Some of these activities can be justified from a motivational point of view, but only a small part of a unit should be allotted to them.

QUESTIONS ON CHAPTER THREE

1._____ True or False: A translation question describes an idea and instructs the student to express the idea in a different form of communication.

2._____ True or False: A fact cannot be translated but a generalization can.

3._____ True or False: A translated answer could take the form of a bulletin board display.

4._____ True or False: It is possible that a student could remember a definition without being able to translate it.

5._____ True or False: In a translation question the teacher is more interested in having students learn the process of translation rather than the ideas to be translated.

6._____ True or False: A translation question can be structured so that a student is asked either to recognize the translation of an idea or to translate an idea himself.

7._____ True or False: A translation question must identify or describe some idea that is to be translated.

8._____ True or False: In the example in this chapter of a sociodrama on the operation of Congress, the students must not be given a detailed description of how a bill becomes a law before they start the dramatization as this would destroy the opportunity to translate.

9._____ True or False: An example of a translation question would be to ask a student to give a literal description of the contents of a picture.

10._____ True or False: Some elementary science texts describe demonstrations of the operation of scientific principles. Students are encouraged to gather necessary equipment and perform the same demonstrations. This illustrates thinking in the translation category.

11. Check the following questions which could lead a person who has read the first three chapters of this book to translate. (You need not answer the questions but only check those that would be classified as translation. Leave the others blank.)

_____A. Define translation in your own words.

_____B. Formulate a translation question for a unit that you teach.

_____C. Construct a graph to present the information in footnote seven of Chapter Two. (Assume the person answering this question knows how to construct a graph).

_____D. Summarize Chapter One. (Assume that the person answering this question knows how to summarize.)

_____E. Classify the questions in a test you have given as calling for "memory" or "more than memory."

12._____ Which of the following two examples illustrates translation?

  A. Question: What is a characteristic of all □'s?
     Answer: This □ is square.
              This □ is square.
              This □ is square.
              This □ is square.
              Therefore all □'s are square.

  B. Question: What is this □?
     Answer: It is a figure that has four straight sides of equal length.

13. How could a teacher present a translation question to a class in a manner to make it unlikely or impossible that a student

would miss it because of inability to remember pertinent information. (Write two or three sentences.)

14. A magazine published a chart giving a great deal of information on a forthcoming election. A teacher assigned a student to reproduce the chart just as shown in the magazine but on a large piece of cardboard so that it would be visible to the entire class. Would you consider this a good translation question for the student who makes the chart? Why? (Answer in two or three sentences.)

RELATING THE TAXONOMY OF QUESTIONS TO A UNIT
OF YOUR CHOICE

15. Write your own list of characteristics of translation questions. Make it in a form that will be a handy reference to use while composing questions. (This question might be stated: "Translate translation.")

16. Use the subject matter and skills that you have chosen for emphasis in your unit to write five or more translation questions.

ANSWERS TO QUESTIONS ON
CHAPTER THREE

1. True.
2. False.   Both facts and generalizations can be translated.
3. True.   This does not mean that every bulletin board display put up by students is an example of translation.
4. True.   This is one reason for asking translation questions.
5. False.   The process is secondary in translation.
6. True.
7. True.
8. False.   A sociodrama on the translation level requires a detailed explanation of the ideas to be translated. A good sociodrama can leave important decisions to the students, but the problem then calls for a higher level of thinking than translation.
9. True.
10. True.   The words "same demonstrations" in the question are meant to imply that no problems are left unanswered in the description in the book. However, it is possible for a text to describe a demonstration for students to perform and then

include questions in which the student uses the principles in a new way which he must think out himself.

11. A, C, and D should be checked. In B, the student is asked to use the idea of translation. This requires more than simply restating the meaning of translation. Question E asks students to relate the ideas of "memory" and "more than memory" to new questions. This also is higher than translation. Translation questions will be even easier to identify after studying the higher categories.

12. B.

13. The teacher could permit the students to use the description of the ideas to be translated. For example, suppose the teacher assigns students to draw a series of stick figure pictures that depict the process by which a bill becomes a law. If students must draw the pictures based on their memory of the process, they might make a mistake because of inability to remember rather than inability to translate. If the students are permitted to use a written description of the process, then any error illustrates inability to translate.

14. Enlarging a picture can hardly be called translation. Certainly it isn't good translation because little understanding is required. Perhaps the teacher can justify the assignment by the benefit to the rest of the class. A good translation question could be made by asking the student to point out to the class the kind of information that is to be found on the chart.

FOUR

❖

INTERPRETATION

Definition of Interpretation

INTERPRETATION QUESTIONS ARE DIFFICULT to define, because there are many kinds of thinking in the category and because all higher levels of thinking are refinements or special emphases of intellectual processes found in an embryonic form in interpretation. This shading of boundaries into higher levels of thinking means that the final definition is not complete until the other categories are described.

The essential characteristic of interpretation is that the student *relates* facts, generalizations, definitions, values, and skills. To relate means to discover or use a relationship between two or more ideas. The interpretation question may give two ideas and ask for the relationship between them or it may give one idea and a relationship and ask for another idea that follows from the evidence. The ideas to be related may be simple or complex. The question is made more involved by asking the student to relate a series of ideas in a variety of forms. The six forms of relationships listed below fall in the interpretation category:

1. Comparative relationship (Determining if ideas are identical, similar, different, unrelated, or contradictory)
2. Relationship of implication
3. Relationship of an inductive generalization to supporting evidence
4. Relationship of a value, skill, or definition to an example of its use
5. Numerical relationship
6. Cause and effect relationship

A characteristic of interpretation is that the student discovers or uses relationships on a common-sense level. The emphasis in the question is on finding the relationship among the parts of the subject matter and not on formal understanding of the thought process involved. For example, a student can engage in induction without being able to define the process in logical terms. The difference between a common-sense use of relationships and a more sophisticated understanding serves as one distinction between the interpretation and analysis categories.

In addition to asking the student to relate ideas on a common-sense level, the interpretation category has two other characteristics. The questions are explicit about what the student should do. If a generalization, definition, value, or skill is to be used, it is identified in the question, although the student may be expected to remember its meaning from previous instruction. Interpretation questions ask for a pattern of thinking that can be predicted in advance because there is usually one and never more than a few legitimate intellectual routes to the answer. This means that the question is objective in the sense that there is one or possibly a few correct answers which can be justified beyond a reasonable doubt. The question may be in either the short-answer or essay format.

The next portion of the chapter is organized according to the six kinds of relationships found in interpretation. Each is defined and exemplified by questions. Teachers who have not had special study in logic may feel that the definitions of the "relationship of implication" and the "relationship of an inductive generalization to supporting evidence" are inadequate for full understanding. This is true. The reason that a full definition is not necessary at this point is that questions in this category call for thinking on the common-sense level. The teacher must understand the definitions only to the extent necessary to see the possibilities for composing questions that use each relationship.

Comparative Relationship

Definition: The student determines whether ideas are identical, similar, different, unrelated, or contradictory. The question often asks for evidence to support the answer.

Examples:

1. In this simple form of comparison, students are asked whether two or more ideas are the same or different. For example, in a third-grade unit on comparative regions in the United States, the students are asked: *Is the climate of Rockport, Maine, different or the same as that of Frostproof, Florida?*[1] On a more advanced level, the students are asked: *Do the United States and West Germany have the same or different attitudes toward the question of whether England should be allowed to enter the European Common Market?*

---

[1] The communities mentioned in this question are used as examples in the textbook: Clarence W. Sorensen, *Ways of Our Land* (Morristown, N.J.: Silver Burdett, 1959).

2. Another type of question asks for degrees of similarity. *Which two communities are most similar in the amount of rainfall each year?* (A) *Frostproof, Florida;* (B) *Greenville, Mississippi;* (C) *Window Rock, New Mexico. Which two economies are most similar in the plan for ownership of capital goods?* (A) *English socialism;* (B) *Swedish socialism;* (C) *Soviet communism;* (D) *United States capitalism.* The two examples of this form of question are objective in that each has one correct answer. However, questions in this format can be such that more than one answer can be justified. In this case, the teacher must give credit for all logically defensible answers. If the teacher plans to use this kind of question with several possible answers, it is best to add another part to the question requiring students to present evidence or arguments to justify the answer they choose. The teacher evaluates the answer by determining whether the justification is adequate. This evaluation procedure keeps the question in the objective form characteristic of interpretation.

3. Students can be asked to relate two or more sets of ideas on specified points. After studying the Greek and Roman civilizations, students are instructed: *Compare the two civilizations in regard to religion, architecture, and government.*

4. The process of comparison required in the questions described thus far is simple, because it does not require much mental power to determine whether two ideas are the same or different. If the questions are missed, it is more likely the result of inability to remember the necessary information. The most challenging comparison questions leave it up to the student to determine the topics on which two or more general sets of ideas are comparable. The broader and more complex the ideas involved, the more room there is for ingenuity. Tom Burns Haber demonstrates a sophisticated level of comparison when he seeks to establish the influence of Virgil on the author of *Beowulf* by citing the similarities between the *Aenoid* and *Beowulf*. Perceptive thought is illustrated in the topics in which he finds them comparable:

(1) evenly matched combats; (2) heroic spirit of willingness to conquer or to die; (3) hero appealed to as the ultimate hope; (4) lack of modesty among warriors; (5) hero's striking personal appearance; (6) hero closely allied with his men; (7) hero attended by a faithful companion; (8) hero advised by an elderly counselor; (9) success and defeat dependent upon three factors: God/Jupiter, Fata/Wyrd, and individual courage.[2]

In a secondary school, students might be instructed: *Compare English socialism with Soviet communism. Compare the Articles of Confederation with the United States Constitution.* A difficulty with this kind of question is that if the comparison has any significance the author or the teacher has probably already called it to the attention of the students and the question changes to one of memory. For this reason there are usually more opportunities for comparison questions that ask students to relate a set of ideas in the current unit to a set of ideas studied in a previous unit. This works well in geography units in elementary school: *Compare the use of natural resources in Africa with their use in Europe.* Questions of this nature are particularly good at the end of the school year when students are able to take a broad view of the subject matter studied during the year.

History teachers have numerous opportunities to ask comparison questions. After studying United States history through the Civil War, students might be instructed: *Compare the relations between the English colonies in North America and England from 1750 to 1783 with the relations between the states and federal government in the United States from 1789 to 1865.* With a question of this type, it is often wise to permit students to use their books as they may have forgotten much of the information from the earlier period in history. In addition, it is unreasonable to expect answers of high quality unless students are given plenty of time to ponder the problem.

Historians like to have students relate a situation from the past

[2] John Nist, "Beowulf and the Classical Epics," *College English*, January, 1963, p. 257.

to the present. This is a good procedure provided that they know enough about the subject on the contemporary scene. In a unit dealing with the United States in the years preceding the Civil War, the students learn of the position of the Negro in society. A common question asks for a comparison of the social position of Negroes before the Civil War with that of today. This is a good exercise if students are given a reasonable opportunity to study the Negro in current society; however, the question would be a poor one to spring in an examination. Students cannot be expected to make a good comparison of two sets of ideas, unless they have a reasonable opportunity to be acquainted with both of them.

Relationship of Implication

Definition: An implication is an idea that follows inevitably from specified evidence. If the evidence is true, then the implication must be true. For example, one textbook defines an oligarchy as "rule by the few," an aristocracy as "rule by the best," and democracy as "rule by the many." An implication is that the government of a nation could not at the same time be an oligarchy and a democracy, but it could be an oligarchy and an aristocracy. The thought process in finding an implication is deduction, although in the interpretation category students need not be aware of the thought process except to understand that the answer must follow directly from the evidence. When a student makes a mistake in specifying an implication, the teacher explains the nature of the error in terms of the subject matter rather than thought process.

The possibilities for questions based on finding implications are tremendous, as illustrated in the following examples.

Examples:

1. A high-school class studying a lesson on tariff and trade is given the following paragraph:

The law of comparative advantage states that a nation should export those goods which it can produce cheaply and import those goods which it finds expensive to produce in comparison with other countries. In other words, it is to the advantage of each country to sell to others the products it can produce at a low cost and buy from others the products that are expensive for it to produce. In this way all products are produced at their lowest cost and everybody benefits from the resulting economic efficiency.[3]

The answers to the following questions require the drawing of implications.

A. True or False: Following the law of comparative advantage would probably lead a nation to produce fewer kinds of goods but greater quantities of each kind.

B. True or False: Following the law of comparative advantage would probably make a nation more dependent on other nations.

C. True or False: Following the law of comparative advantage would probably be beneficial for an industrial nation but not for an agricultural nation.

D. True or False: Following the law of comparative advantage would probably reduce trade among nations.

E. True or False: A nation that follows the law of comparative advantage would probably enact a high tariff schedule.

None of these questions is directly answered in the definition of the law of comparative advantage. In each case students infer a logical implication.

The article from the *Senior Scholastic* defining the law of comparative advantage illustrates the difficulties in framing questions calling for implications. The sentences that follow the definition of the law in the magazine destroy the possibility for a whole series of good questions. They read:

But in practice, the levying of tariffs on imports upsets this economic efficiency and the operation of the law.

[3] "U.S. Trade Policies . . . Shackle or Springboard," *Senior Scholastic*, December 6, 1961, p. 11.

Many, in fact, believe that free trade in every commodity would be the best idea because of the law of comparative advantage.[4]

For instructional purposes, it is better for the student to deduce the relationship between tariffs and the law of comparative advantage.

2. Another type of question using implications introduces a new concept that is probably unknown to the student. The thought process requires him to relate new information to knowledge previously learned and to draw an implication.

A. A nation is self-sufficient when it produces all or nearly all the goods it uses. Would following the law of comparative advantage tend to make a nation more or less self-sufficient?

B. The prosperity of some nations in the world depends on a single crop, mineral, or manufactured good. If the price of this product falls, the whole nation suffers economic depression. Would following the law of comparative advantage tend to increase or decrease the number of nations that would depend on a single product?

These two questions have the added advantage that, besides promoting understanding of the law of comparative advantage, they teach that an important concept is related to the topic (self-sufficiency and the one-crop evil).

3. The arguments on tariff can be approached in a way that produces good interpretation questions featuring the drawing of implications. Two partisan statements on the problem are presented to the students. In this example, the positions are brought before the class in the form of a movie entitled *World Trade for Better Living* which favors low tariffs and a speech advocating high tariffs given by Congressman C. M. Bailey. Excerpts from these two sources are presented below followed by questions calling for the drawing of implications.

Statements from the movie *World Trade for Better Living:*

[4] *Loc. cit.*

High tariffs, quotas, and embargoes don't make sense.

The more goods we produce and exchange, the more goods we have to consume and the higher the standard of living.

I suppose it is natural for people to want protection against competition. But when it comes to foreign trade you want to remember that we sell to other nations as well as buy from them. When we ask for higher tariffs then people in other countries do the same and won't buy our goods.

In other words, let's raise the productivity everywhere and let every nation give us the things it can produce best.[5]

Statements from a speech by Congressman C. M. Bailey:

Now a standard of living can be high or it can be low. Fortunately we have had a high one. When tariffs go down imports go up—a truism with which there can be no argument. Sales suffer first, then jobs, and then the factory itself. The latter may either go bankrupt or 'get out of town'—in this case out of the country to a manufacturing facility abroad.

What happens then to the 'standard of living' in the original domestic location. Let me take a recent example. On August 20, a release was carried in the newspapers that the Remington Rand Co., manufacturers of typewriters in Elmira, New York, would soon discontinue domestic production and transfer their activities to Europe. The release indicated that about 3,000 employees would be laid off.

What now happens to the 'standard of living' in Elmira, a city of 45,000 persons. Foreign imports of portable typewriters, bound duty-free by GATT in 1951 has increased from 22,000 to 318,000 in 1958—a 1,400% increase. Meanwhile our exports dropped 80% from 313,000 to only 56,000 during the same period. In 1959 imports had 43% of the U.S. market and our share of the world market dropped from 63% to 7% since 1948.

In crude petroleum production, U.S. output from 1950 to 1959 increased from 1.9 billion barrels to only 2.5 billion while non-U.S. production jumped from 3.8 billion to over 7 billion barrels. Therefore, the U.S. portion of world production dropped from 52% in 1950 to 36% in 1959.[6]

[5] *World Trade for Better Living*, Encyclopaedia Britannica Film.
[6] Cleveland M. Bailey, "Foreign Competition," *Vital Speeches*, November 15, 1960, pp. 73–76.

A. What explanation or justification would the authors of the movie give concerning the lowering standard of living in Elmira?

B. How might the authors of the movie interpret the figures on the crude oil production differently in order to support their case?

C. Which of the two sides has the more nationalistic argument?

Relationship of an Inductive Generalization to Supporting Evidence

Definition: A scholar draws an inductive conclusion when he observes that many members of a class of things have a common characteristic and then concludes that all members of the class must have the same characteristic. For example, an anthropologist studying a culture may notice that the children are strictly controlled by the parents. When he sees the same phenomenon in many families with no or few exceptions, he may decide that the evidence justifies the inductive conclusion that strict parental discipline of children is a characteristic of the culture. An inductive generalization differs from an implication in that the latter starts with facts and generalizations and seeks new conclusions that are entailed within them, while the former requires a marshalling of evidence about some members of a class with the object of finding a characteristic of all members, including the ones not observed. A properly-drawn implication is beyond serious doubt, while an inductive conclusion can never be accepted as certain. In the case of the anthropologist's conclusion, it may be that he accidentally observed only families with a certain parent-child relationship or it may be that the parents controlled their children strictly only when strangers were present.

Full use of induction does not fall in the interpretation category, partly because this kind of thinking does not produce objective conclusions and partly because it requires formal training. Induction is a splendid kind of thinking, but in education it is most useful in the analysis category.

Example:

There is one kind of interpretation question that requires the ability to see a relationship between an inductive conclusion and supporting evidence. The student is given an inductive conclusion and asked to find or to recognize evidence that supports it: *Find evidence in your textbook that supports or refutes these generalizations: (A) The moral character of man is slowly improving. (B) Power corrupts and absolute power corrupts absolutely. (C) The United States has a depression every thirty years.* The object of the question is not to prove or disprove the generalization, but rather to recognize evidence that relates to the truth or falsity of the generalization. The difficulty of the question can be adjusted to the maturity of the students. Following are generalizations appropriate for a sixth-grade class studying western culture and geography: *(A) Great civilizations have not developed in the tropics. (B) There was no freedom in the ancient world.* Questions of this sort are most appropriate at the end of a unit or at the end of the school year. The students then can look back over sweeping segments of familiar subject matter to find the necessary evidence.

Relationship of a Value, Skill, or Definition to an Example of Its Use

Definition: The student is given a value, skill, or definition and asked to identify or compose an example of its use.

When a value is used in the interpretation category, the student is not asked to make an evaluation but rather to recognize the use of the value. A higher category called evaluation requires the use of values to make judgments.

Examples (using values):
The following exercise is designed for an eighth-grade Civil War unit:

Directions: Following are five kinds of arguments:
1. Arguments based on selfish advantage
2. Arguments based on the idea that other people believe the same thing
3. Arguments that have little or nothing to do with the problem
4. Arguments based on Judeo-Christian and/or democratic values
5. Arguments based on false facts or ideas

Following are some arguments for and against slavery. Classify each as an example of one or more of the five kinds of arguments listed above.

1. Slavery is right because it has existed through most of history.
2. ". . . it is as much the order of nature that men should enslave each other as that animals should prey upon each other."
3. In the years before the Civil War, the slaves of the South were treated as well as or better than the factory workers of the North.
4. Slavery is wrong because it existed primarily in the South.
5. I should not have to give up my slaves because they cost me over $1000 each.
6. Slavery is right because it was accepted by the men who wrote the United States Constitution.
7. Slavery is wrong because it violates the idea that all men are created equal.
8. Slavery is a just system because Negroes need the guidance of the superior white race.
9. Slavery is right because it was supported by the great Greek, Aristotle.
10. Negroes have weak minds. Nature has made them suitable only for slavery.

11. Slavery is wrong because all men should have an opportunity to develop their full talents.

Example (using a skill):

The following exercise consists of a description of the skill of comparing ideas followed by interpretation questions asking the student to demonstrate his ability to use the skill. Social studies teachers often present problems like the following to their classes: (A) *Compare Alexander Hamilton's beliefs concerning the proper role of government with those of Thomas Jefferson.* (B) *In what ways does Soviet communism follow and depart from the plan for an ideal communist society described by Karl Marx?* (C) *Compare this article from the* National Review *with this article from* The Reporter.

The intellectual process of comparison is more complicated than it appears on the surface. Ideas can be identical, similar, different, unrelated, or contradictory. When comparing two sets of ideas, such as two magazine articles, it is possible to make both general and specific comparisons. For example, two articles might generally agree but be different on specific points. In addition, one article is likely to consider aspects of the subject not considered in the other.

The first step in making a comparison is to master the ideas to be compared. This requires study and note-taking. The student must determine topics that are common to the two sets of ideas and the ways in which specific points are related. The next step is to organize the presentation of the comparison. Following are three ways a comparison can be made.

First Way to Compare A and B
1. Introduce the subject discussed in the articles.
2. Identify a topic discussed in both articles and compare the position of the two.
3. Identify another topic discussed in both articles and compare the position of the two.

4. Identify all other topics discussed in both articles and compare them.
5. Make a general summation of the comparison of the two articles.

Second Way to Compare A and B
1. Introduce the subject discussed in the articles.
2. Discuss all ways in which the two articles are identical or similar.
3. Discuss all ways in which the two articles are different or contradictory.
4. Make a general summation of the comparison of the two articles.

Third Way to Compare A and B
1. Introduce the subject discussed in the articles.
2. Summarize one article.
3. Summarize the other article.
4. Point out specific ways in which the two articles are related.
5. Make a general summation of the comparison of the two articles.

In the last example, a frequent error is to skip IV and V. *In making a comparison, it is not enough to summarize the two sets of ideas.* Even when the comparisons seem obvious, they must be explicitly pointed out. The person making a comparison must perform the whole process and not leave part of the responsibility to the reader.

The next section completes the description of the skill by comparing the ideas in two articles using the "First Way to Compare A and B." The two articles are given to the students at this point, but they are omitted here due to their length. They are: "Rights Lost to Big Government," by Barry M. Goldwater,[7] and

[7] *Chicago American*, November 8, 1962.

"The Myth and Reality In Our National Economy" (excerpts), by John F. Kennedy.[8]

President Kennedy and Senator Goldwater evaluate the role of the national government in these articles.

Topic 1:   The two men disagree in their thinking on governmental growth. Goldwater writes about "the prodigious growth of federal authority" and cites examples of the increasing powers assumed by the national government. Kennedy discusses this problem mainly from the viewpoint of federal expenditures and notes that, while the money spent by the government has tended to increase with time, if defense and space spending are ignored, the national government is growing less rapidly than private business and industry.

Topic 2:   The two men partially agree on the effect of national government on individual freedom. Both cite the laws in agriculture as examples of increasing federal control. Kennedy, however, makes the point that federal action does not necessarily mean federal control, and he uses the example of the appropriations for scientific research without damage to the independence of scientists. He states that there is a danger from big government but also there are advantages.

Topic 3:   Senator Goldwater asserts that constitutional limitations on government are being violated. He also believes that the actions of the government in such fields as agriculture and labor-management relations have been bungling efforts. As evidence of confusion, he notes that the national government simultaneously proposes a balanced budget and expensive projects which doom a balanced budget. President Kennedy does not specifically deal with these charges in this article.

Summary: The President terms the idea that national government is big and bad as a "myth." Senator Goldwater vehemently disagrees.

Two kinds of questions follow the instruction in the skill of comparison. In the first kind, the teacher presents faulty comparisons and asks the student to identify the errors. In the second, the student is given the more challenging task of making his own

[8] *Vital Speeches*, July 15, 1962, p. 579.

comparisons of two sets of ideas. Following are examples of interpretation questions requiring students to demonstrate skill in comparisons:

1. Compare the national platforms of the Republican and Democratic Parties in 1964.
2. Compare the current foreign policy of the Soviet Union with that of the Chinese communists.
3. Compare Martin Luther King's plan to promote the interests of Negroes in the United States with Booker T. Washington's plan.
4. Compare the reaction to automation of the railroad unions with that of coal mining unions.

These questions cover a variety of topics; in practice, however, it is efficient to relate skills to specific units of study. Thus, skill in comparison might be emphasized in a labor-management unit.

Examples (using definitions):

The use of definitions in an eighth-grade unit on the Civil War makes up the next exercise. The formal study of semantics belongs in the analysis category, but some elementary problems on the meaning of words are best classified as interpretation. The students are given the following definitions[9] and examples of the use of words and then asked questions requiring them to use the knowledge:

civil war: War . . . "occurring within the state or between citizens. . . ."
revolt: "An outbreak . . . against established authority"
revolution: "A change . . . that involves the overthrow . . . of an existing government . . . and the establishment of a new government; a successful revolt . . ."
rebel: ". . . one who resists any authority or control; one who refuses to obey or to submit. . . ."

[9] Reprinted from *Funk & Wagnalls New Standard Dictionary of the English Language,* Copyright 1963, by permission of the publishers, Funk & Wagnalls Company, Inc.

rebellion: ". . . organized resistance, by force and arms to the
              . . . government, by those who owe it obedience"

Examples of special uses of some of the words:

1. In 1789 the French people killed their king and set up a new
   government that was first democratic in many ways but later
   fell under the dictatorial influence of Napoleon. This is called
   the French *Revolution*.
2. In 1936 army officers in Spain overthrew the Spanish Republic
   and after several years of fighting established a dictatorship
   under Franco. This is called the Spanish *Civil War*.
3. Northerners sometimes call the *Civil War* in the United States
   the War of the *Rebellion*.
4. Without any bloodshed the English people forced their king
   to leave the nation in 1688 and then they set up a more democratic government. This is called the Glorious *Revolution*.
5. The American colonies of England won their independence in
   the *Revolutionary* War.
6. In the United States, the South declared its independence in
   1861 but, after four years of fighting, were forced back into
   the Union. This is called the *Civil War*.

Questions to be answered by students:

1. Why would it be incorrect to give the name "Southern Revolution" to the part of our history that is usually called the
   Civil War?
2. Is it correct to call the winning of independence of a colony
   from the mother country a revolution?
3. Is it correct to call a war between two independent countries
   a revolution?
4. Is it correct to call a war that takes place between two groups
   in one country a civil war?
5. The soldiers on one side of the Civil War were called rebels.
   Which side would you think it would be?
6. Must a revolution involve fighting?

7. Could the French Revolution correctly be called a civil war? a revolt? a rebellion?

8. Could the Spanish Civil War correctly be called a revolt? a rebellion? a revolution?

9. Could the Glorious Revolution correctly be called a civil war? a revolt? a rebellion?

10. Do you know another use of the word "revolution" which does not involve an overthrow of a government?

11. What civil wars do you know about that are going on in the world now?

12. Why is it unreasonable to call a war a revolution until it is completed?

Quantitative Relationship

Definition: Numerical concepts have a precision that makes them ideal building material for stimulating questions. On the interpretation level, the student is asked to use statistical information to draw conclusions. Questions seldom require the students to do more than simple arithmetic because the object of the question is not primarily to test mathematical skill but rather to give the student practice in drawing conclusions from statistical evidence.

Example:

The main objective in the following exercise is to have students discover statistical relationships significant to important fiscal problems of the United States government. Questions 1 and 2 in Part I call for translation. The last parts of Questions 4 and 8 and Question 11 in Part II call for evaluation; the remainder require the student to interpret using quantitative relationships.

Considerations on public fiscal policies· Should taxes be cut? Is the government going bankrupt? Every citizen who grapples with these questions should first study the evidence.

YEAR	FEDERAL SPENDING IN BILLIONS OF DOLLARS	SURPLUS OR DEFICIT IN BILLIONS OF DOLLARS	NATIONAL DEBT AT END OF YEAR IN BILLIONS OF DOLLARS	GROSS NATIONAL PRODUCT IN BILLIONS OF DOLLARS	POPULA- TION IN MILLIONS OF PEOPLE	CORPO- RATE DEBT AS PERCENT OF GNP
1945	98.4	−54.0	258.7	213.6	139.9	46.6
1946	60.4	−20.7	269.4	210.7	141.4	51.9
1947	39.0	0.7	258.3	234.3	144.1	54.7
1948	32.9	8.4	252.3	259.4	146.6	53.5
1949	39.5	−1.8	252.7	284.6	149.2	56.7
1950	39.5	−3.1	257.4	329.0	151.7	58.7
1951	44.0	3.5	255.2	329.0	154.4	57.9
1952	65.3	−4.0	259.1	347.0	157.0	58.1
1953	74.1	−9.4	266.1	365.4	159.6	57.9
1954	67.5	−3.1	271.3	363.1	162.4	59.6
1955	64.4	−4.1	274.4	397.5	165.3	63.1
1956	66.2	1.6	272.8	419.2	168.2	65.6
1957	69.0	1.6	270.5	442.8	171.2	66.3
1958	71.3	−2.8	276.3	444.5	174.2	69.6
1959	80.3	−12.4	284.7	482.8	177.1	69.6
1960	76.5	1.2	286.3	504.4	179.3	69.8
1961	81.5	−3.8	289.2	520.1	185.0	
1962	87.7	−6.3	298.6	550.0[a]	187.0	
1963	94.3[a]	−8.8[a]	307.4[a]	573.0[a]		
1964	99.8[b]	−11.9[b]	319.3[b]	600.0[b]		

[a] Estimated.   [b] Predicted or proposed.

PART I: Use the above statistics to make the following graphs:

1. Make a graph that plots federal spending from 1945 to 1963.
2. Make a graph that plots the national debt from 1945 to 1963.
3. Make a graph that shows what percentage of the gross national product federal spending has been each year from 1945 to 1963.
4. Make a graph that shows what percentage of the gross national product the national debt has been from 1945 to 1963.
5. Make a graph that shows how much federal spending has been per person per year from 1945 to 1963.

6. Make a graph that shows each person's share of the national debt during each year from 1945 to 1963.

7. Make a graph that compares the national debt as a percentage of the gross national product with the corporate debt as a percentage of the gross national product from 1945 to 1960.

PART II: Use the graphs to answer these questions:

1. Has federal spending as an absolute increased or decreased since 1945? since 1948? How much?

2. As a percentage of gross national product, has federal spending increased or decreased since 1945? since 1948? How much?

3. Has federal spending per person per year increased or decreased since 1945? since 1948? How much?

4. In what ways do the answers to Questions 2 and 3 give a different view of federal spending than the answer to Question 1? Which view is more meaningful? Why?

5. Has the national debt as an absolute increased or decreased since 1945? How much?

6. Has the national debt as a percentage of gross national product increased or decreased since 1945? How much?

7. Has each person's share of the national debt increased or decreased since 1945? How much?

8. In what ways do the answers to Questions 6 and 7 give a different view of the national debt than the answer to Question 5? Which view is more meaningful? Why?

9. What conclusions might be drawn from the graph in 7 in Part I?

10. What factors other than those presented here should be included in considerations of public fiscal policy?

11. In light of the experience you have gained in this exercise, what advice would you give to citizens considering public fiscal policy?

This exercise is designed for secondary-school students, but quantitative interpretation in the social studies should be started in the elementary school.

Cause and Effect Relationship

Definition: Our culture accepts the idea that there is an explanation for every happening and the factors responsible for any phenomenon are called causes. The assignment of causes and effects is a common mental process in everyday life, but it is a more precarious operation than most people suspect. Modern scholars usually find multiple causes and seldom are satisfied with a verdict such as that pronounced by historian James F. Rhodes when he declared slavery to be *the* cause of the Civil War. An intensive study of cause and effect is reserved for the analysis category, but the subject is considered on a layman's level in interpretation.

Example:

The following lesson is to be presented orally by the teacher to a class of eighth-grade students as an introduction to the study of the causes of the Civil War.

A cause, according to one dictionary, is "anything that produces an effect or result." A cause makes something happen. Sometimes causes seem simple. I push a book—like this—and it moves. (Demonstrate.) The effect is the movement of the book. What is the cause of the movement of the book? I can think of four possibilities. Perhaps you can think of others. (Write on blackboard.)

1. I caused it.
2. My finger caused it.
3. My arm muscles caused it.
4. Energy from the food I ate caused it.

Which causes seem to include others? Which do you believe to be the best explanation and why?

Suppose a man is required by his boss to work until 2:00 A.M. to complete a job. While driving home from work, he falls asleep at the wheel and runs into a tree. What caused the accident? How many reasonable causes can you suggest? (List on board.)

Do you think that the causes of the Civil War would be more or less complicated than the causes of this auto accident? Why?

In view of this discussion, which of the following statements (written on the board) about the causes of the Civil War do you believe to be the *most accurate* description of what we will discover when we study this subject?

1. There is one cause of the Civil War.
2. Historians agree on the cause or causes of the Civil War.
3. One man's guess as to the cause or causes of the Civil War is as good as the next.
4. The cause or causes of the Civil War are complicated.
5. The careful study of history can help us to a more accurate understanding of the cause or causes of the Civil War.
6. No historian can prove without a shadow of a doubt that his interpretation of the cause or causes of the Civil War is the correct one.

Questions using the word "why" often ask for a cause in a manner that is understandable even to the youngest students. The problem with this kind of question is that it is difficult to present it in a context in which the student actually surmises the cause.

More ideas on cause and effect are presented in the chapter on analysis.

Interpretation Questions Based on the Format of the Question

The best approach to defining interpretation questions is the one used up to this point—that is, through the consideration of thought processes. A second approach—the description of the format of the question—is used in this section to illustrate the analogy, the irrelevant item, and the scrambled outline. These three kinds of questions lead the student to interpret if the answers have not been revealed in previous instruction.

The analogy question requires the student to make an inference in the basic pattern of A is to B as _____ is to D. In a good analogy, A and B are related to each other in the same way as are C and D. In addition, B should be in the same class as D. For example: *The President is to the United States government as the _____ is to the government of Great Britain.* The student's thinking should go something like this: "What is the relationship of a President to the United States government? He is the highest executive officer. Great Britain and the United States are both nations; so the answer must be the highest executive officer of Great Britain which is the Prime Minister."

┌────── Both top executive officers ──────┐
The President is to the United States as the Prime Minister is to
                                          Great Britain.
└── Both nations ──┘

There are many variations of the basic pattern for an analogy question.

A is to B as C is to _____.
A is to B as _____ is to D, as _____ is to F, etc.
A and B are to C, as D and E are to _____.
A but not B is to C, as D but not _____ is to F.

A wide range of complexity makes the analogy appropriate for all grade levels. *The engineer is to the locomotive as the _____ is to the airplane. Zeno is to stoicism as _____ is to existentialism.*

Faulty analogies are easy to compose, because the relationships among the parts are not explicit in either the question or the answer. In the question: *The President is to the United States government as the _____ is to the government of Great Britain,* a student might answer "the Queen" and be technically correct, because the President of the United States serves a ceremonial function in the same manner as does the Queen of England. The teacher may be tempted to mark "the Queen" as wrong, "because we didn't study about her" or "because the Prime Minister is a better answer." When composing the question, the teacher should consciously identify the relationship and satisfy himself that it is not too tenuous. One helpful technique is to make the more general class into the unknown. Another is to ask students to identify the relationship as part of the answer. *The President is to the United States government as the _____ is to the government of Great Britain. What relationship does the President have to the United States that your answer shares with Great Britain?* The precaution of making the general term into the unknown is violated here, but the second part of the question allows the student to justify an answer other than Prime Minister.

Analogy questions should not be sprung on students for the first time in an examination. Teachers should explain the nature of an analogy and give practice in class. After this preparation, new analogy questions can be asked in the examination.

To write an irrelevant-item question, the teacher finds a series of related ideas and adds an irrelevant item that appears superficially plausible. A final United States history examination could include this question: *Which date does not fit in this group?* (A) *1812;* (B) *1824;* (C) *1914;* (D) *1941.* The student is expected to reason that all dates except 1824 mark the beginning of a war fought by the United States. If the question follows sources of information used in instruction too closely, it does not really call for interpretation. For example, suppose the text contained descriptions of Jefferson's and Hamilton's attitudes toward government. If the teacher lists three of Jefferson's attitudes and one of Hamilton's in an irrelevant-item question, the student can determine the answer by memory alone.

The irrelevant-item question has strengths and weaknesses similar to the analogy. In a Civil War unit, students were instructed: *Identify the state that does not fit in the following list:* (A) *Missouri;* (B) *Maryland;* (C) *Kentucky;* (D) *Maine.* The relationship the teacher sought was that three were border states in the conflict and one was not. Several students chose Kentucky as the correct answer, because the other three started with "M." Technically, the students answered the question accurately, but the teacher is justified in marking their answers wrong because it is far off the subject. In several instances in this chapter, it is noted that a teacher must accept *reasonable* answers he has not anticipated. However, students must understand that there is a limit as to what is reasonable.

Students frequently answer questions about individual points in a reading assignment and yet are not able to visualize the ideas in a unified whole. The scrambled outline asks them to see the forest as well as the trees.

Directions: The following ideas from your reading assignment fit logically into the outline. Enter each one in its proper position:

Reasons why bases are of declining importance
Development of long-range missiles
Power to strike back helps prevent attack
Reasons for increasing opposition to American bases overseas
Rising nationalism in foreign countries
Increasing neutralism
Development of Polaris submarine
Bases in Turkey made possible quick action in Lebanon
South Korea probably would have been lost without bases in Japan
Preparation to deal with small local wars
Threats by communists
Reasons why the United States must keep bases

   I.
      A.
      B.
      C.
  II.
      A.
      B.
        1.
        2.
III.
      A.
      B.

In composing this kind of question, the teacher writes an outline of a reading assignment and then scrambles the various points. The first thing the student must do is to pick out the main points. In the above question they are: "Reasons why bases are of declining importance;" "Reasons for increasing opposition to American bases overseas;" and "Reasons why the United States must keep bases." Sometimes the main points fall into a natural sequence, but not in this case. The next step is to put the related subheadings under each main heading. The pattern for the subheadings reveals the way in which the ideas fit into the outline.

I. Reasons for increasing opposition to American bases
    A. Rising nationalism in foreign countries
    B. Increasing neutralism
    C. Threats by Communists
II. Reasons why the United States must keep bases
    A. Power to strike back helps prevent attack
    B. Preparation to deal with small local wars
        1. South Korea probably would be lost without bases in Japan
        2. Bases in Turkey made possible quick action in Lebanon
III. Reasons why bases are of declining importance
    A. Development of long-range missiles
    B. Development of Polaris

In correcting this exercise, some leeway is possible. For example, there is no reason why points IA, IB, and IC could not be interchanged. The same is true for IIIA and IIIB, and also IIB1 and IIB2.

Another version of the scrambled outline follows this pattern:

Directions: The following ideas from your reading assignment fit into the outline in several ways. Do not enter them but answer Questions 1 through 3.

a. North Atlantic Treaty Organization
b. Alliances designed to prevent expansion of Red China
c. Southeast Asia Treaty Organization
d. Containment through collective security
e. Central Treaty Organization
f. Alliances designed to prevent expansion of Soviet Uuion
g. ANZUS Pact

Title _____

I.
   A.
   B.
II.
   A.
   B.

1. What is the letter of the idea listed above that best serves as the title of the outline?
2. If Item B under II is "North Atlantic Treaty Organization," what is the letter of the only topic that would fit logically in I?
3. If Item B under II is "Southeast Asia Treaty Organization," what is the letter of the only topic that would fit logically in A under II?

Instruction in the elements of organization of ideas can be started in the earliest years of school. Two kindergarten teachers presented a unit on milk production to their classes. As one of the culminating activities, the children were asked to arrange a series of pictures to show the proper sequence of events. The seven pictures had not been seen previously by the class. (A) Cows in pasture; (B) Farmer milking; (C) Farmer pouring milk in cooler; (D) Truck going to dairy; (E) Bottling of milk; (F) Milkman delivering to home; (G) Child drinking milk. This problem is similar to the earlier ones in that students are asked to fit separate ideas into a whole.

A teacher may have several objectives in mind when he asks interpretation questions. A student who is able to *relate* ideas demonstrates a higher mastery than one who only recalls them. For example, a student comparing the New Deal with the Square Deal shows a higher level of comprehension than one who can only describe the two. Drawing relationships between two or more ideas may lead the student to discover vital knowledge. A comparison of the principles of fascism with the principles underlying government of the Soviet Union today reveals striking similarities between supposedly conflicting ideologies. A hypothesis of this book is that if a student discovers this kind of relationship, the knowledge is more firmly fixed in his mind than if he memorizes the comparisons made by others. Interpretation questions lead students into intellectual processes too often reserved for scholars, authors, and teachers.

QUESTIONS ON CHAPTER FOUR

1. _____ The verb that best sums up the mental process of interpretation is: (A) remember; (B) relate; (C) rehearse; (D) recognize.
2. _____ Which one of the following is *not* a characteristic of interpretation questions? (A) The question is in short-answer format. (B) The question deals with thinking on a common-sense level rather than on the basis of conscious understanding of the formal logic involved. (C) The question requires students to form, recognize, or use a relationship. (D) The question has one or possibly a few correct answers. (E) The question is specific about what a student is to do and also about the ideas with which he is to work.
3. _____ True or False: A student can arrive at a deductive conclusion without being conscious that he is performing a mental operation defined as deduction.
4. _____ True or False: An interpretation question often includes some information new to the student.
5. The ideas listed below are from this chapter and fit logically into the blanks of the outline following them. Enter each idea in its proper position. There is some leeway in the answer. For example, IA1 through IA6 need not be in any special order.

Irrelevant item
Cause and effect relationship
Interpretation questions based on the format of the question
Usually only one correct answer
Explicit about that which is to be answered
Numerical relationship
Relationship of a value, skill, or definition to an example of its use
Scrambled outline
Relationship of implication
Comparative relationship
Essential characteristics of interpretation
Analogy
Answer made on common-sense level

Problem requires discovery, identification, or use of a relationship

Relationship of an inductive generalization to supporting evidence

I.
   A.
      1.
      2.
      3.
      4.
      5.
      6.
   B.
   C.
   D.
II.
   A.
   B.
   C.

6. Which one or more of the six relationships used in interpretation are illustrated in each of the questions that follow? (See the first page of Chapter Four for the relationships. You may answer by the number of the relationship.)

_____ A. (After a chronological study of American history) Compare the machinery of the League of Nations for keeping the peace with that of the United Nations.

_____ B. (After a chronological study of American history in which the meaning of the phrase "peace without victory" is related to the history of World War I but not to World War II) To what extent did the United States use the concept of "peace without victory" after World War II?

_____ C. (After providing students with a list of the qualities of a good oral report) Present a report to the class on the Black Muslims.

_____ D. (After providing necessary statistical data in chart form) Did the average of industrial wages or did the prices of consumer goods increase more rapidly in the United States from 1865 to 1900?

7. An eleventh-grade American history class has just completed the study of the period of history in which the United States

Constitution was written. As an examination question the teacher asks, "How did the concept of democracy held by Madison, Hamilton, and Jay differ from the common meaning of the concept today?" What possible weakness do you see in this question? (Write one or two sentences.)

8. A common kind of question asks the student to assume the role of a certain person or member of a group in writing an answer. An assignment might be: "Pretend you are the editor of a western newspaper in 1850. Write an editorial describing your probable attitude toward the federal land policy." Assume that the student's text presents a description of how westerners feel about the disposition of federal land. Would you classify the assignment as memory, translation, or interpretation? (Tell why in one or two sentences.)

9. Classify each of the following questions as "memory," "translation," or "interpretation." (Assume that the person who is to answer the question has read the first four chapters of this book.)

_____A. Name the six forms of relationships that are made in the interpretation category.

_____B. Under which of the six forms of relationships in interpretation might the thinking in the translation category be classified?

_____C. True or False: A question that requires finding a numerical relationship might at the same time require finding a comparative relationship.

_____D. Explain in your own words the meaning of "relationship of an inductive generalization to supporting evidence."

_____E. Compose a question requiring the students to find the relationship of an inductive generalization to supporting evidence.

_____F. What are the main characteristics of a question in the interpretation category?

10. This chapter points out that an interpretation question often introduces a new idea and asks students to relate it to something they have studied. Each of the four parts of this question presents a new idea. Use the four new ideas to write four interpretation questions appropriate for someone to answer who is studying the taxonomy of questions.

A. A dictionary gives the definition of "taxonomy" as "the

science of classification; laws and principles covering the classification of objects."

B. Following is a paragraph from a book assigned to be read by a ninth-grade citizenship class:

"The British do not have a written constitution, nor do they have a system of states' rights. Yet Britain is a democracy. British democracy has a system of balanced rights and divided authority. A British government must consider the views of many individuals and organized bodies before it can act. Parliament seems to rule, but it is actually the people who rule through Parliament."[10]

The teacher of this citizenship class asked the following questions based on this passage:

1. Does Britain have a constitution?
2. Is Britain a democracy?
3. Britain has a system of _____ rights and _____ authority. (Fill in the blanks.)
4. Who actually rules Britain?

C. "A school devoted to routines, to dull repetition of the traditional form of assign-study-recite, will likely produce thinkers only as individuals revolt against the dreary round."[11]

D. A distinction has been made between convergent and divergent thinking. Convergent thinking is prompted by a problem in which the given evidence points in the direction of a single correct answer. Divergent thinking results from a problem where there are many correct responses. An example of a question leading to convergent thinking is: *Classify this question on the taxonomy of questions.* A divergent question is: *Write a divergent question.*

RELATING THE TAXONOMY OF QUESTIONS TO A UNIT OF YOUR CHOICE

11. Write your own list of characteristics of interpretation questions. Make it in a form that will be a handy reference to use while composing questions.

[10] Editors of Scholastic Magazines, *What You Should Know About Democracy and Why* (New York: Scholastic Book Services, 1964) p. 15.
[11] William Burton *et al.*, *Education for Effective Thinking* (New York: Appleton-Century-Crofts, 1960) p. 52.

12. Write ten or more interpretation questions using the subject matter of your unit. The interpretation category provides a greater variety and volume of questions than any other and is deserving of much practice. Try to write a number of different kinds of interpretation questions. Use any additional subject matter you need to develop them.

ANSWERS TO QUESTIONS ON
CHAPTER FOUR

1. B.
2. A.
3. True.
4. True.
5. (The items within each bracket are interchangeable.)
   I. Essential characteristics of interpretation
      A. Problem requires discovery, identification, or use of a generalization
         1. Comparative relationship
         2. Relationship of implication
         3. Relationship of an inductive generalization to supporting evidence
         4. Relationship of a value, skill, or definition to an example of its use
         5. Numerical relationship
         6. Cause and effect relationship
      B. Usually only one correct answer
      C. Explicit about that which is to be answered
      D. Answer made on common-sense level
   II. Interpretation questions based on the format of the question
      A. Analogy
      B. Irrelevant item
      C. Scrambled outline
6. A, 1; B, 4; C, 4; D, 5 or 2 or 1.
   Part B illustrates the use of a definition. Part C illustrates use of the skill in presenting on oral report. The student who reports on the Black Muslims might do other interpretive thinking too, but we cannot know this from the evidence given. Part D brings out the idea that a numerical relationship will also take the form of one or more other relationships.

7. This question is a weak one if students have not studied the contemporary meaning of democracy. (Perhaps readers will detect other weaknesses.)

8. This question has the characteristics of translation but in reality calls for the same answer as, "How did westerners feel about federal land policy in 1850?" Test writers often assume that this kind of question requires more reasoning than it really does.

9. A. Memory;   B. Interpretation;   C. Interpretation;   D. Translation; (This is one of the kinds of questions that fall in the misty flats between memory and translation. Either answer can be justified.)   E. Interpretation; (This question leans in the direction of the higher category of synthesis. To be more clearly interpretation, it should have suggested the inductive generalization with which the person who answers the question should work.);   F. Memory.

10. There are other possibilities for interpretation questions than the examples suggested in these answers.

   A. 1. Compare the dictionary definition of "taxonomy" with the definition given in Chapter One.
   2. True or False: According to the dictionary definition of taxonomy, a classification system need not be cumulative and sequential.

   B. 1. Classify the questions asked by the teacher.
   2. Write an interpretation question based upon the information given in the paragraph.

   C. 1. True or False: "Assign-study-recite" can refer only to questions in the memory category.

   D. 1. Does interpretation best illustrate convergent or divergent thinking?
   2. Could a memory question be divergent?
   3. Would convergent or divergent questions allow more room for creativeness?
   4. Check the following questions that are divergent.
      _____ a. True or False: Interpretation questions can and usually do require the student to remember as well as to interpret.
      _____ b. Name all categories that can include memory in answering a question.
      _____ c. Create a new system for classifying questions.

FIVE

❖

APPLICATION

Definition of Application

EDUCATION SHOULD BE PREPARATION for life; but, in fact, it is often artificial and far removed from reality. Application questions present problems that approximate the form and context in which they would be encountered in life. In an era of rapid change, educators are concerned about preparing students for life in an unknown future. The application category of questions is designed to give students practice in the transfer of training.

There are three main characteristics of the questions in the application category. First, these questions deal with knowledge which has explanatory or problem-solving power. This is the kind of knowledge that is transferable to many new situations. Second, they deal with the whole of ideas and skills rather than solely with the parts. In the early stages of the instruction of a complicated skill or pattern of ideas, a teacher divides the intellectual process and knowledge into simple segments. This is sound procedure if it is followed by application questions asking the student to reassemble the ideas and skills into their natural whole. The third characteristic is that application questions include a minimum of directions or instructions, because the questions are based on previous learning and the student is expected to know what to do. When a student meets a problem in life, there will be no teacher present to give directions. Application questions give practice in independent use of knowledge and skills.

An application question can be built from a simple principle, definition, value, or skill. For example, one elementary text contains a unit on health in which the students learn the principle that body temperature often rises when a person is ill. A couple of chapters later in a unit on heat, there is a picture of a group of children sitting around a table. The sun is shining through the window on one boy and he appears flushed. The students are asked the question: "Why do you think Johnny is so warm?" The answer sought is that he is sitting in the sun. At that point the teacher could ask the application question: "Can you think of another reason which might explain why Johnny looks warmer than the other children?" This is an application question because it asks the student to use a principle studied earlier in a new and unexpected context. The second characteristic of application questions—that of dealing with whole ideas—is not a factor in this case, because the principle relating fever to illness is so simple that it was never broken into parts.

More often, an application question focuses on a *pattern* of principles, definitions, values, and skills. At the beginning of the year, one civics teacher presents a list of ten principles of United States government to his students as part of a unit on the federal government. First, each principle is studied separately, but soon students are expected to be able to use the whole list. Through the year the content of the course moves through state and local government, and students are asked to apply the principles to each new topic. The most common form of question is to present a new political situation and ask the student to explain the way in which one or more principles are illustrated or violated. This question asks for the use of a whole pattern of ideas—the principles of government. However, the question tips off what is to be done in a way that partially violates the third characteristic of application—that of giving a minimum of directions. This is unavoidable, because a fair question on the use of the principles cannot be formulated without telling the pupils to use the principles. More often than not an application question partly violates one of its characteristics as it is difficult to reproduce life-like problems in the classroom.

Not all generalizations, definitions, values, or skills can or should be used in application questions. Some ideas are related to so few new situations that they are not applicable. Application questions always deal with ideas that have been studied previously and there is not enough time to rethink everything on the application level. In addition, it is unrealistic to expect students to be constantly prepared to apply any idea studied previously. The main criterion for selecting ideas for application is their importance.

Students will be successful with application questions only if prepared for them. The teacher should explain why application questions are necessary. For example, at the time the civics teacher presents the ten principles of American government, he might say something like this: "These principles are so important that they are a theme of the whole course. I am giving you fair warning now that I will present questions unexpectedly through the year in which you will be asked to use the principles." Another fair way to use application questions is in oral questions to the class. The example of the application of the idea that a rise in body temperature is often a sign of illness was presented orally. The student who reasoned the answer could be given special credit, but it would be unfair to penalize those who did not perceive which principle applied.

The distinction between application and interpretation centers on the instructional context in which a question is asked. A lesson on the "frustration-aggression theory" might feature interpretation questions asking students to recognize or compose examples of the operation of the theory. The context of learning is one in which the students know that they are expected to use this theory. At the end of a unit or at the end of the year, the teacher offers an application question requiring the same kind of reasoning, except that it does not explicitly say the solution requires the use of the frustration-aggression theory. The student is expected to perceive that the use of the theory is called for implicitly by the problem. The authors of the *Taxonomy of Educational Objectives* summarize the differences between application and interpretation thus:

A problem in the . . . (interpretation) category requires the student to know an abstraction well enough that he can correctly demonstrate its use when specifically asked to do so. "Application," however, requires a step beyond this. Given a problem new to the student, he will apply the appropriate abstraction without having to be prompted as to which abstraction is correct or without having to be shown how to use it in that situation.[1]

In some subject fields, application questions are obvious and frequently used. For example, in bookkeeping, students normally study one operation at a time. On one day the "balance sheet" is the subject for attention, and, after proper instruction, the teacher presents an interpretation problem requiring the use of the balance sheet. On another day the same instructional procedure would be followed with the "profit and loss statement." Near the end of the course when students have mastered all basic knowledge and processes separately, the teacher presents a "practice set." This is in the form of the records of a mythical business

[1] Benjamin S. Bloom (ed.), *Taxonomy of Educational Objectives* (New York: Longmans, Green, 1956), p. 120.

concern and includes transactions the student must enter into the records. The problem is similar to one the student might encounter in life as a bookkeeper.

The professional education of a teacher presents an example of application in the form of practice teaching. This experience follows the formal instruction in curriculum, teaching methods, and psychology of learning. The ability to answer questions on these subjects is not the same experience as applying the ideas in a classroom full of supercharged pupils. Other subject fields in which application questions are often used are language arts, industrial arts, mathematics, physical education, and music.[2]

The social studies present special problems in the application category. Part of the difficulty is related to the controversy over the definition of "social studies." Some define the phrase broadly as the study of human behavior, while others who are more subject-minded define social studies as a combination of the disciplines of history, geography, political science, economics, and sociology. The controversy is much more involved than can be described here and there is a broad middle ground. The point is that one of the manifestations of this controversy is a difference of opinion on application questions. Those who conceive of social studies as the study of human behavior advocate a greater emphasis on encouraging students to engage in real-life social experiences. This position is illustrated in the following quotation from a pamphlet published by the Citizenship Education Project. "Indeed, it is really what the citizen *does* with what he knows and thinks that counts. If citizenship is an active thing, then it must be taught through action."[3] Subject matter is not ignored, but it is clear that the authors believe an education is incomplete if it

[2] The distinction made in the next three paragraphs between "behavior-centered application" and "subject-centered application" is irrelevant for non-social studies teachers. However, the examples of application questions presented under each of these titles later in the chapter are useful to any teacher in illustrating the nature of application questions.

[3] From *Improving Citizenship Education* by Citizenship Education Project © 1952 Teacher's College, Columbia University, p. 3. Used by permission of McGraw-Hill Book Company.

concentrates on the intellectual mastery of subject matter and stops short of action.

Critics of this behavior-centered approach point to frothy units in "social living" featuring instruction on asking a girl for a date. They note that students who engage in a "get-out-the-vote" campaign spend so much time in organizing car pools and baby-sitting services they may be unaware of campaign issues. The subject-minded teachers point to evidence that citizens of the United States have a pathetically small amount of knowledge of history and other social studies. A commitment to action in public projects is harmful to the general welfare of students if they act without deep understanding of the nature of the problem.

Many educators are struck by the fact that both sides of this controversy have some convincing arguments and that within our current understanding of learning the best position lies somewhere in the middle. Whichever position a teacher endorses, application questions of certain types are appropriate for his classroom. In the case of the behavior-centered teacher, there are real-life problems or projects requiring students to participate in situations commonly faced by citizens. For the subject-centered teacher, there are questions focusing primarily on intellectual processes used by scholars to find order and significance in their discipline.

Behavior-Centered Application

1. One of the best thought-out plans for behavior-centered application problems is the Citizenship Education Project of Columbia University. This program defines an instructional procedure called a "laboratory practice" which is designed to teach citizenship. In a laboratory practice, students study and take action on problems of their school and community. The criteria for a laboratory practice are these: It must be real, have focus, have purpose, involve gathering firsthand information and taking

action. These criteria are spelled out in detail and are illustrated in the following example:

ATTACKING THE TRAFFIC PROBLEM

SUMMARY OF THE PRACTICE:

Students decided to try to bring about a traffic improvement local people had been talking about for years. They wanted to eliminate a serious bottleneck where a crowded parkway intersected one of their city's main thoroughfares. They made a survey of merchants', pedestrians', and car owners' opinion; tabulated the number of accidents; interviewed a traffic officer and City Council members. They took pictures documenting hazards. They presented a petition based on all this evidence to the City Council, which acted on their recommendation. The former bottleneck is now an efficient one-way street.

THIS WAS A LABORATORY PRACTICE BECAUSE:

It Was Real

Students tackled a serious traffic problem in the community. They took active roles as real citizens.

It Had Focus

Students concentrated their efforts on getting something done about a particular traffic problem. Then their job was done.

It Had Purpose

It highlighted the importance of participating in public affairs and the rights and responsibilities of citizens. It also taught the structure and function of local government.

It Included Gathering Information Firsthand

Students found out what merchants, pedestrians, and car owners wanted done; collected statistics regarding accidents; interviewed traffic officers and City Council members; took pictures.

It Involved Students in Taking Action

As they gathered and documented the material for their report, presented their report to traffic officers and finally to the City

Council, students were *serving their community*. They were also engaged in *influencing others* as they pressed to get their recommendation accepted.[4]

The materials for the Citizenship Education Project include over one hundred recommended projects, such as: setting up a youth traffic court; conducting a national citizenship day program; forming Young Democrats and Young Republicans Clubs in the school; raising funds for international relief; and forming a civil defense medical team. Many activities are also recommended for subject fields other than the social studies.

Part of this program suggests ways to tie each activity to important subject matter. A card file presents sources of pertinent information dealing with every recommended laboratory practice. One pamphlet entitled *Premises of American Liberty* gives an excellent summary of the basic democratic values of our nation which students can relate to their particular problems.[5] In summary, the Citizenship Education Project anticipates the potential weaknesses of behavior-centered learning and recommends procedures whereby they can be minimized or avoided.

2. As was pointed out in Chapter One, the taxonomy of questions deals with the intellectual side of behavior rather than the emotional. The weakness of this arbitrary division shows up in the application, synthesis, and evaluation categories, because attitudes often play an important role in all three. A behavior-centered project illustrating concern for attitudes is reported in *The Bulletin of the National Association of Secondary-School Principals*.[6] This project grew out of a plan for observance of Brotherhood Week in a girls' school in New York. By chance the students' attention was drawn to an incident in which a Negro

[4] Citizenship Education Project, *What Is A Laboratory Practice* (New York: Teachers College, Columbia University, 1953), p. 20.
[5] Citizenship Education Project, *Premises of American Liberty* (New York: Teachers College, Columbia University, 1952).
[6] Carl Cherkes and Theresa Held, "Translating Social Studies Concepts into Action," *The Bulletin of the National Association of Secondary-School Principals,* September, 1961, pp. 85–90.

mother faced the wrath of segregationists in order to enroll her child in school. The courage of the mother and child captured the admiration of the students and led ultimately to a scholarship for the child and a Woman of the Year Award to the mother, which was presented to her in person in a school assembly. Virtually the whole school participated in the planning and executing of the elaborate project. In assessing the outcome, a teacher wrote:

We destroyed the wall of academic indifference that some girls had built around themselves. When the indifferent student became aware that what was printed between the covers of a book was related to what took place in the classroom, and what took place in the classroom was related to what was taking place in the world, there was a marked improvement in attitude and performance.[7]

The original problem of how to observe Brotherhood Week resolved into two kinds of intellectual activities. The first was the mastery of subject matter in regard to the false doctrine concerning race. The second was planning and executing the project. Some of the questions that must have arisen were these: *How can we raise money for the scholarship and for the transportation of the mother and child to New York? Where will they stay while in New York? Who will make posters and talk to the press about publicity?* This last kind of question takes a great deal of time and is criticized by the subject-centered teacher as being outside the proper domain of the social studies. The behavior-centered educator answers that a project of this type often is more likely to influence behavior and to motivate more serious study than a unit involving only the use of information from books.

3. A form of sociodrama was described earlier as an example of translation. With different organization the procedure also fits into the application category. One common example is to have students dramatize the operation of a governing body, such as the United Nations General Assembly. First, they must study the

[7] *Ibid.*, p. 89.

operation of the organization and some of the issues facing it. Next, an agenda is chosen and each student assigned to play the part of a representative of a particular nation. This is followed by a period of research in which students discover how their nations would logically react to the chosen issues, so that in the actual debate they can play their roles accurately. At the conclusion of the drama, the teacher or class can evaluate the success of each student in playing his role.

A similar procedure is used in many citizenship classes when students take over the offices of the local government for a day. Economics students might dramatize a collective bargaining session in one of the publicized labor-management struggles. History students could dramatize any one of the famous assemblies of the past, such as the Congress of Vienna. Projects of this type can easily misrepresent the truth unless based on a thorough study of the real event.

4. The members of the Student Council and the class officers of a school are supposedly given opportunities to practice rights and responsibilities of leadership, but too often their functions are executed in a manner that distorts the purpose. The Student Council sometimes does little more than serve as a front through which the school administration funnels unpopular regulations. An election is supposed to involve a reasoned choice based on a knowledge of the responsibilities of the office and qualifications of the candidates, but school elections are seldom conducted on any other basis than social popularity.

Subject-Centered Application

The subject-centered educator considers application thinking to be important in education, but he defines the process with a strong intellectual emphasis. Following are examples of intellectual behaviors that can be learned through practice with application questions:

1. An educated person possesses a framework of knowledge into which new information can be categorized. For example, when a man reads about "managed news" he automatically relates it to basic political concepts of free press and the right of the public to have information about the operation of the government. He also relates it to other political philosophies that compete with our system.
2. An educated person understands and uses the specialized vocabulary of the social sciences.
3. An educated person is aware of all major controversial issues and relates new information to the arguments on either side.
4. An educated person knows how to find information on important matters. He uses the library skillfully. He listens intelligently and observes perceptively.
5. An educated person can express himself effectively in oral and written form on social issues.[8]

In every case the educated man is doing something that should be practiced in a fruitful, intellectual life. One kind of application question asks students to practice these mental processes as preparation for life. Following are examples:

1. In a ninth-grade citizenship course, students learn the basic principles of American government and also the principles of the American version of capitalism. In this question they relate these principles to a description of the mythical nation of Alpha.

Directions: Write an essay on the ways the imaginary nation of Alpha (described below) follows or violates the basic principles of the United States government and the principles of modified capitalism. Analyze only the situation in Alpha as it is under the new government—not as it was under General Napoleon.

[8] Several important behaviors of an educated person are omitted from this list, because they emphasize thought processes that are considered in higher categories of thought. They would include these: 6. An educated man avoids errors in logical reasoning and recognizes sound or weak logic in the thinking of others. 7. An educated man is creative. 8. An educated man recognizes value judgments and treats them appropriately.

The imaginary nation of Alpha recently had a revolution that overthrew the dictatorial government of General Napoleon. The crimes of the General were so numerous and cruel that he was condemned to death after a trial that lasted only one-half hour.

The 100 army officers who led the revolution declared that the new government would be a people's democracy. A legislature made up of two houses was established. The House of Delegates and the House of Peers each has 50 members elected by a majority vote of the adult citizens. Any citizen over 25 years of age may run for the House of Delegates, but the membership of the House of Peers must be chosen from the 100 army officers who led the revolution. A bill may originate in either house, but both houses must approve a bill before it becomes law. The executive powers are assigned to a cabinet which is elected by the legislature from among its members. The legislature also appoints the Supreme Court, which can declare laws unconstitutional.

The newly written Constitution of Alpha defines the rights of the people and the powers of the government. Free speech, free press, free assembly, and free choice of religion are the rights of all citizens. One exception is that nobody may speak or write anything that advocates the return of the political party formerly headed by General Napoleon. A special court tries all political cases.

The nation of Alpha is divided into 25 geographical districts called departments. Each department has an elected legislature that may pass laws for the district. However, the national legislature can veto any law passed by the departments that are not in the public interest. Laws passed by the departments are of lesser importance, because the Constitution gives almost all political power to the national government.

Under the government of General Napoleon, the standard of living of the common people in Alpha was low. A few wealthy people owned most of the land and capital goods. One of the first acts of the new legislature was to enact a law that no person could own more than 2000 acres of land. All owners of more than this minimum were paid a fair price for the land that they gave up. The land was sold to peasants at a low price and with a 25-year mortgage.

Under the government of General Napoleon there had been a ten percent tax on personal income and no corporation taxes. The new government enacted a graduated tax on personal income starting with one percent for incomes over $500, and up to fifty percent on incomes over $300,000. A tax was also levied on corporated income but with provisions that encouraged private investment and expansion of industries. Inheritance taxes were low. The legislature is spending a substantial portion of the tax revenue in building schools. Current plans call for six years of free education for all children.

The question on Alpha follows all characteristics of the application category. First, it is related to life because in these days of competing political and economic ideologies it is important for a citizen to be able to make an assessment of the positions of other nations. The question would be better if it described a real nation—perhaps one of the African countries. The advantage of using a mythical nation is that it is easier for the teacher to invent a situation than to find information on a nation that would suit the needs of the question. Second, the question deals with whole sets of ideas rather than small parts. Third, the question is not overly explicit about the directions, because students are expected to know what to do as a result of previous instruction. They should know the principles involved and the standards for an appropriate essay. Another variation would be to assign a research project in which students choose a nation, gather pertinent information about the political and economic system, and then compare it with the system in the United States.

2. Application questions stressing the use of subject matter can be used in the lower grades too. A third-grade book by Clarence W. Sorensen entitled *Ways of Our Land* emphasizes the following ideas:[9]

A. The people in the United States live in many different ways.
B. The land and weather vary in the nation and influence the lives of the people.
C. The people of our nation specialize in certain kinds of production. This makes higher productivity possible.
D. Transportation is necessary for exchange of products.

[9] Clarence W. Sorensen, *Ways of Our Land* (Morristown, N.J.: Silver Burdett, 1959).

E. The use of machines makes possible greater production of
   goods.

At the end of the year, the teacher might read to the students
the following passage without any introductory comments:

In our social studies class this year, we studied about many
parts of our country. I'm going to read the names of the communities we visited. As I read, you think of what you remember
about the community and people: (slowly) Rockport, Maine;
Frostproof, Florida; Greenville, Mississippi; Nemacolin, Pennsylvania; Lake Geneva, Wisconsin; Amarillo, Texas; Window Rock,
Arizona; San Francisco, California; and Shetlar, Washington. All
these communities are in our country, the United States of
America. Today I would like to tell you about another country far
away. When I finish describing this new country, I will ask you
how it is the same as the United States and how it is different.
(This question is a facade to cover the main purpose of the exercise which is to have the children detect the contradiction of
the main ideas studied during the year.)

The country we will study has the strange name of Beta. Here
is the way it looks on a map. (Have it on a large poster or on the
blackboard in colored chalk.) The middle part of the country is
dry and mountainous. Sometimes it does not rain all year. The
part next to the ocean is flat land that gets plenty of rainfall, but
some land is more fertile than other land. The black dots are the
cities and the star the capital.

Beta doesn't have any coal or other valuable minerals under
the ground. The ocean is full of fish, but the people don't like the
taste of fish so they do not try to catch them. The people of this
country make their living by growing wheat. Every family plows
its own fields, sows the wheat, and reaps the crop at the end of
the summer. Almost all farming is done by hand or with the aid
of horses. Because everyone grows wheat, there is little need to
exchange products and there are few railroads, airplanes, ships,
or even automobiles.

The people in Beta love peace and fear war. The leaders
noticed that other countries are almost always fighting. The President decided that his country could stay out of war by keeping
all people at home and not allowing the citizens from other nations to come to Beta, even for purposes of trading.

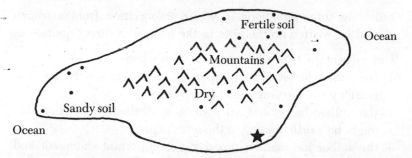

The homes of the people in Beta are much like those in our community. Most of them have telephones, radios, refrigerators, and television sets. The children go to school and at this very minute some may be studying about life in our community.

Now tell me how Beta is much the same as the United States and how it is different.

The students will probably offer some of the similarities and differences. However, the main point is that the teacher hopes the students will challenge the following violations of the main principles taught during the entire year:

1. Everyone grows wheat, including people in areas not suited to it.
2. The people have an abundant material life without the use of productive machines or specialization.
3. The people produce only wheat but, even without foreign trade, use all kinds of goods.

Application of Skills

In previous chapters, skills are discussed on the memory and interpretation levels. The mastery of skills is not complete until the student uses them successfully in the application category. Following is an example of the transition in the use of a skill from memory to application. Suppose a teacher is instructing a class of high-school students in the techniques of taking research notes for a term paper. As a part of this instruction, he might offer the following three situations in which information from a source should be written on the note in the form of a direct quotation:

Use a direct quote in your research notes when:

1. the author has stated an important idea so concisely that you cannot write the same thing in fewer words;
2. the author has stated an idea in a distinctive manner that might be worth quoting in the term paper;
3. the author has made a surprising or important statement and you wish to preserve the proof that he said it;

On the memory level, the teacher would ask, *What are three situations in which you would quote the words of an author directly into your research notes?* To test interpretation, a teacher could devise a problem, such as the following:

Directions: Imagine that you are writing a term paper on arguments for and against the direct primary. You come upon the following article by Senator Proxmire in which he states his position. Write the statements from the article that should be quoted in your research notes. After each statement you select, tell why you believe the statement should be quoted. (These directions would be followed by a mimeographed copy of the article.)

Application requires carrying the skill through another step. After instruction is given in all aspects of writing a term paper, the student writes one of his own. As a part of the evaluation of the project, the teacher asks to see the student's research notes to determine whether he has followed sound procedure in the use of research skills, including the extraction and use of direct quotations. It is discouraging to note how often a student will be able to answer memory and interpretation questions on each aspect of a functional idea or skill and then fail to apply the idea or skill when he has occasion to use it in a broad context.

The research paper or oral report based upon research fulfills all characteristics of the application category. It is a usable skill, because most people are confronted by situations in which they are called upon to make a detailed study of a subject and present the information, along with conclusions, to some audience. A salesman must know his products thoroughly in order to present his case to his customer. A home owner may need to study city zoning in order to protect his property values. The member of a civic or fraternal organization or of a church may be called upon to make reports of various kinds. The process involved in each of these cases follows many of the same general procedures as a research paper. Besides having practical value, the research paper or oral presentation requires students to select appropriate skills from the "whole" of research methodology and apply them to a specific case. The amount of direction that the teacher gives can easily be adjusted to the maturity of the student. At the highest level, the teacher should have to assign very little more than the general subject. The student should know that he must follow these general procedures:

I. Define the topic
   A. Select a topic within the competency of writer
   B. Select a topic of manageable dimensions
   C. Select a topic with opportunities for originality

II. Locate information
   A. Use various sources of information
     1. Card catalogue
     2. General reference books dealing with social studies
     3. Vertical file
     4. *Readers' Guide to Periodical Literature*
     5. Sources of information outside the library
   B. Read skillfully
     1. Extensive reading
     2. Intensive reading

III. Take information onto notes
   A. Write bibliography cards
   B. Know the characteristics of a good note
     1. Information necessary on each note
     2. Direct quotations
     3. Paraphrases

IV. Analyze information in sources
   A. Distinguish between relevant and irrelevant information
   B. Assess the quality of sources of information
   C. Distinguish facts from opinions (evaluation category)
   D. Recognize valid and invalid reasoning (analysis category)
   E. Compare information from different sources
   F. Draw justifiable conclusions in relation to topic or problem of the paper

 V. Organize the ideas
   A. Know the meaning of organization
   B. Know the patterns for organization
      1. Chronological
      2. By process
      3. Cause and effect
      4. Topical

VI. Write the paper
   A. Prepare the tentative outline
   B. Arrange notes according to outline
   C. Write the rough draft
      1. Introduction
      2. Body
      3. Conclusion
   D. Rewrite
   E. Prepare the footnotes and bibliography
   F. Proofread

This general outline includes many important skills in the social studies. It is noteworthy, however, that almost all the skills involved are not within the exclusive domain of the social studies but must be taught in coordination with other subject fields. The outline also emphasizes the great breadth and complexity of the skills involved. Most students are not prepared to write a research paper as outlined above until they are near the end of high school. However, in an earlier grade they may be given problems that have the characteristics of application for their level of development. Students in the upper elementary grades are often assigned projects in which they gather and present information. After proper instruction on the memory and interpretation levels, they can be assigned a simple report that calls for locating information, paraphrasing ideas, organizing ideas into an outline, and writing or orally presenting the report. For students in the upper elementary school, this amounts to application at the level of responsibility appropriate to them.

The great difficulty in coordinating the efforts of many teachers in different subject fields and grade levels is the chief impediment in preparing students to conduct sound research. This is primarily a problem of curriculum development and requires a workable definition of responsibility in skill development at each grade level. The taxonomy of questions can be helpful in providing the definition, because it offers a framework for the description of skills at increasing levels of complexity.

QUESTIONS ON CHAPTER FIVE

1.____ True or False: An idea should be taught on lower levels than application before it is practiced on the application level.

2.____ True or False: A student might be able to use a concept when he is told to do so in a specific situation but not be able to recognize when the concept is applicable.

3.____ True or False: Application questions normally are asked at the beginning of a unit or of a school year.

4.____ True or False: An idea taught and evaluated in one unit on the interpretation level can often be evaluated again in a subsequent unit on the application level.

5.____ True or False: An application question is more explicit about directions than is an interpretation question.

6.____ True or False: An illustration of application thinking is the case in which a student uses learning from his mathematics in the construction of a project in industrial arts.

7._____ True or False: There is often a factor of student attitude in the application category. A student may learn rules of grammar in English but feel that they are unimportant in social studies and therefore ignore them.

8._____ True or False: Application questions ask students to be able to use an idea without explicitly telling them to do so.

9._____ True or False: After students have determined which idea is appropriate to solve an application problem, the remainder of the thinking is similar to that found in lower categories.

10._____ True or False: A teacher presents an application question when he describes a process and then follows it with a problem in which the process is to be used.

11._____ True or False: In an application question the teacher attempts to present a problem as near as possible to the way in which the problem might be encountered in life.

12._____ True or False: One difficulty in writing application questions is in structuring a problem that calls for the use of a skill or generalization but does not overtly reveal which skill or generalization is to be used in arriving at the solution.

13._____ Is the teacher who makes the following statement having difficulty in his own thinking on the interpretation level or on the application level? (For your answer write either "interpretation" or "application.")

The teacher states, "If somebody designates appropriate subject matter and asks me to formulate an application question, I can do so. However, I have difficulty finding the opportunities for application questions in the units I teach."

14. Determine whether each of the following descriptions of questions best illustrates "interpretation" or "application":

_____A. A student of the taxonomy is asked to determine whether a group of questions best illustrates interpretation or application.

_____B. After studying the interpretation category of questions, a student of the taxonomy is asked to compose a question that exhibits the qualities of interpretation.

_____C. The student of the taxonomy is given a chapter from a text and asked to compose questions.

_____D. A student of the taxonomy recognizes an opportunity to ask an interpretation question.

_____E. The student of the taxonomy is asked to study some of the tests he has given during the year and identify application questions he has asked.

15. How could the following question be changed so that it would ask for application thinking?

The accompanying paragraph (one to be chosen by the teacher) contains errors in the use of capital letters, commas, semicolons and periods. Correct the errors.

16. Some generalizations are more widely usable than others in making life understandable. What significance does this have in writing application questions? (Write two or three sentences.)

17. Why does our rapidly changing world make application questions so important? (Write one or two sentences.)

RELATING THE TAXONOMY OF QUESTIONS TO A UNIT
OF YOUR CHOICE

18. Write your own list of characteristics of application questions to serve as a reference.

19. Write five or more application questions for your unit. In this category it is necessary to specify briefly the manner in which the idea or skill was originally presented to the student and the context in which the application question will be asked.

ANSWERS TO QUESTIONS ON
CHAPTER FIVE

1. True.
2. True.
3. False.
4. True.
5. False.
6. True.
7. True.
8. True.
9. True.
10. False.

11. True.
12. True.
13. Application.
14. A. Interpretation; (The directions are too specific to be application. Also, the student is asked to deal with only two out of the seven categories.) B. Interpretation; C. Application; (This is as close to pure application as can be structured for these ideas in a classroom. It deals with all kinds of questions —the whole idea—and is not overly explicit about directions.) D. Application; (This is the purest illustration of application of this series, but it is one which really happened in life rather than being contrived for classroom use.) E. Interpretation; (The whole pattern of questions is not used and the directions are too explicit for application.)
15. The question should be less definite about the kinds of errors to be corrected. In the application form the question could read: "Correct the errors in this paragraph."
16. One of the factors that can make a generalization important is widespread usability. In addition, if the generalization has many uses, it will be easier to find situations in which it can be practiced and evaluated.
17. If the world is changing rapidly, the best preparation for the future is practice in the use of generalizations, definitions, skills, and values that will be meaningful in many new situations.

SIX

❖

ANALYSIS

Definition of Analysis

IN ALL CATEGORIES, except analysis, a teacher can immediately apply the ideas on questioning to his classroom. Analysis is different in that the thinking is relatively unfamiliar to many teachers and cannot be used until it is mastered on a deeper level than is possible to describe in this chapter. The purpose of defining and illustrating analysis is to show how it fits into the taxonomy of questions and to encourage teachers to investigate a form of question that this author believes deserves more attention on all grade levels. After completing this chapter, the reader should know the characteristics of analysis and be able to recognize analysis questions. This is all that is necessary to comprehend and

97

use the higher categories of synthesis and evaluation. A teacher who wishes to develop understandings necessary to use analysis questions in his classroom may refer to the books cited at the end of the chapter.

The distinctive feature of the analysis category is that it requires solutions of problems in the light of conscious knowledge of the parts and processes of reasoning. In interpretation and application, the emphasis is on using subject matter to arrive at conclusions but without special attention by the student as to how it is done. For example, the definition of interpretation states that the category includes both induction and deduction, but the thinker does not have to know the definition or nature of these forms of thought. In analysis, there continues to be a concern for subject matter; but, in addition, the student must be conscious of the intellectual process he is performing and know the rules for reaching a valid and true conclusion.

There are four main sources of ideas on reasoning in the social studies. One is in the methodology developed for each scholastic discipline, such as the historical method and the geographic method. These methodologies consist of careful appraisals of the processes whereby knowledge in the subject is discovered and used. The second source is the fountainhead of information on reasoning—the discipline of logic and its sister subject semantics. Very little formal logic finds its way into the curriculum. This is unfortunate because training in reasoning is among the most important goals in education. A third source of information is the description of propaganda techniques, such as those suggested by The Institute for Propaganda Analysis in *The Fine Art of Propaganda*.[1] Last, the *Taxonomy of Educational Objectives* provides a system for studying reasoning. This list does not exhaust all sources on the subject, but it includes the best. A marginal source is the study of the rules of evidence used in courts to establish guilt, innocence, and equity.

---

[1] The Institute for Propaganda Analysis, *The Fine Art of Propaganda* (New York: Harcourt, Brace & World, 1937).

The difference between the common-sense reasoning in the interpretation and application categories on the one hand· and the more sophisticated form in the analysis category on the other is illustrated in the variance between the answers to the following problems:

1. *Tell why the reasoning in the following quotation is sound or unsound: Mr. X wants to be elected to Congress. Do you remember that he worked overseas in our giveaway foreign aid program? Everyone knows there have been proven cases of corruption in the administration of mutual security funds. Let's not elect a crook to Congress.* On the interpretation level, this could be answered thus: "The conclusion is not sound, because not everyone dealing in foreign aid was dishonest. The argument does not prove that Mr. X is either honest or dishonest." On the analysis level, the answer goes further: "The argument takes the form of a categorical syllogism.

Major Premise: All who participate in the foreign aid program
                 are corrupt.
Minor Premise: Mr. X participated in the foreign aid program.
Conclusion: Mr. X is corrupt.

The conclusion is valid, according to the rules of logic, but the major premise in the argument is unsubstantiated and subject to doubt; so the truth of the conclusion is not proven or disproven."

2. *Tell why the reasoning in the following quotation is sound or unsound: Statistical studies show that students who own automobiles have substantially lower grades in high school than students who do not own them. Nothing is more important to high-school youth than to receive a good education; so students should not own automobiles.* An interpreted answer might question the source of the statistics and argue that there are important aspects of life for young people other than formal education. Some advantages of automobile ownership could also be offered to cast doubt on the conclusion drawn in the quotation. The analyzed answer would cover the same points but would go further in

identifying the parts and forms of the argument: "The argument offers a generalization that was apparently inductively formulated by comparing grades of students who owned automobiles with those who did not. Not enough information is offered to determine the quality of the generalization. Even if it is properly drawn, the speaker has no right to assume that the cause of low grades is automobile ownership, because this represents the *post hoc* fallacy. It is possible that low grades in school cause students to buy automobiles in an effort to gain recognition that does not come to them in the classroom. The value judgment that education is the most important aspect in the lives of young people is combined with the alleged cause of poor grades to arrive at the conclusion that high-school students should not own automobiles. The conclusion is valid but unproven because of the uncertainty of the premises."

Attention to the parts and processes of reasoning in analysis does not make an absolutely clear division with interpretation and application, because the latter two cannot be performed without some *elementary* knowledge of the components of thought. Common words in a layman's vocabulary are: proof, truth, fact, reason, conclusion, evidence, definition, cause, effect, comparison, relationship, and propaganda. These words are used frequently in interpretation and application questions with the expectation that students will know their meaning—at least at the level of common usage. Analysis thinking is based upon a more sophisticated understanding of these common ideas and on a knowledge of other less obvious ideas about the forms of subject matter and the nature of reasoning. The line between the layman's knowledge and the sophisticated understanding of the parts and processes of reasoning is indistinct. It is not important for the classroom teacher to be able to locate this line but it is important that he use appropriate knowledge and questions on both sides of the line.

Another distinction between analysis and interpretation is that the latter is much more explicit about what is to be done and about the subject matter and skills needed to answer the question. Because analysis appears above application in the taxonomy hierarchy, it includes the characteristics of application. This means that an analysis question is posed in a format similar to that in which the problem might be encountered outside the classroom. The most common form of analysis question offers an example of reasoning and instructs the student to analyze it. The question does not explicitly ask the student to find a fallacy or to test the quality of deduction. On the basis of previous instruction, the student is expected to know the kind of reasoning involved and that he should test the validity of the arguments according to appropriate rules of reasoning.[2]

Analysis questions are generally neglected in the social studies. This is not surprising, because, for the most part, this kind of thinking has been reserved for scholars and only they have needed to give serious attention to the parts and processes of reasoning in their disciplines. With the contention that students should participate to a greater extent in the thinking in every discipline, it becomes vital for them to learn more of the process. So little has been done with this in the past that a good deal of study and experimentation is necessary to determine at which levels various forms of analysis should be introduced and refined in the curriculum and how analysis can best be taught. The next few pages present an exploration of possible approaches to the parts and processes of reasoning under the topics of induction, fallacies, deduction, and semantics. *The brief descriptions are designed only to introduce some possibilities of the subjects. A*

---

[2] The definition of analysis offered in this chapter is narrower and more precise than the one suggested by Bloom. The *Taxonomy of Educational Objectives* defines analysis thus: "The breakdown of a communication into its constituent elements or parts such that the relative hierarchy of ideas is made clear and/or the relations between the ideas expressed are made explicit. Such analyses are intended to clarify the communication, to indicate how the communication is organized, and the way in which it manages to convey its effects, as well as its basis and arrangement." (p. 205).

This definition is weak because it overlaps the interpretation category and does not emphasize the great value to be derived from explicitly relating the thinking in the analysis category to well-conceived systems of reasoning.

far deeper understanding is necessary for teachers who wish to integrate analysis into the curriculum.

Induction

Induction involves reasoning from the specific to the general. The sequence of thinking is to observe characteristics of many members of a class and then generalize about the characteristics of all other unobserved members. Because we observe that the length of daylight hours waxes and wanes with the passage of the seasons, we generalize that this will continue to happen in the future. Because men in the past have all died, we infer that men will continue to die. Because every yellow perch we examine can live only under water, we generalize that this is the characteristic of all yellow perch. Induction, then, takes the form of examining the qualities of some members of a class and proclaiming that all other unexamined members of the class will have the same characteristics.

If the observer accurately examines every member of a class and generalizes his observation, the conclusion is certainly true. For example, after a complete examination, a person might generalize: "Every pair of socks I own has at least one hole." This is tabulation rather than induction. Real induction requires generalization based on observation of only *some* members of a class. As such, an inductive conclusion never can be considered true beyond a doubt. However, we can have more confidence in some inductive generalizations than in others, depending on the quality and volume of supporting evidence. Books dealing with induction provide standards for the evaluation of the quality of an inducted generalization. One book lists these:

1. "The criterion of number of instances"
   In general, the more instances observed, the more confidence can be placed in the conclusion.

2. "No contrary instances"

   The induction is destroyed or weakened by contrary instances. If one immortal man is discovered, it destroys the generalization that man is mortal. Sometimes we formulate generalizations that are not destroyed by a single or limited number of exceptions. The existence of a few albino robins does not completely undermine the usefulness of the inductive generalization that robins have rufous-colored breasts.

3. "Nonvariable character of the phenomenon under investigation"

   Although there is no known instances of a yellow perch being able to survive out of water, the confidence in this generalization is slightly weakened by the fact that another fish (the lungfish) is able to survive in both water and air. The generalization "man is mortal" has more reliability, because all living things eventually die.

4. "Independent confirmation by deduction from more general laws"

   The generalization that the sun rises every day can be formulated by observation. An astronomer can also give good evidence that the sun should rise every day without relying wholly on observation, because the periodic rising of the sun follows from other astronomical knowledge.[3]

There are other aspects of induction that could profitably be taught in the schools. Students can learn to observe accurately and to judge the reliability of witnesses. The whole realm of subjective factors in thinking is worthy of consideration. The hazards of selecting a sampling in induction can be taught and practiced. The nature of hypotheses and theories and the means of composing and testing them should be studied as should the theories on the nature of truth. The idea of probability is often considered in mathematics, but it also has significance in the physical and

---

[3] Joseph G. Brennan, *A Handbook of Logic* (New York: Harper & Row, 1961), pp. 179–184.

social sciences. The use of analogy in argument and the relationship between cause and effect are worthy of special attention. A comparison of the problems of induction when applied to the physical and social sciences is an important understanding to be mastered by students.

Fallacies

The most common mistakes in reasoning have been identified by logicians and called "fallacies." Most fallacies are easy to understand and are a valuable tool in everyday life as well as in formal education. A study of them could be brought into the curriculum in a sequence of steps starting in the elementary grades. The ninth-grade citizenship course would be an ideal place for emphasis on errors in reasoning, and, by the end of the year, students should know the most common fallacies by name and be able to recognize them. The curriculum of the last three years of high school should provide students the opportunities to demonstrate their ability to identify fallacies and avoid them in reasoning.

In a classroom that centers on memorization of the textbook, students do not encounter illogical thinking, because it is carefully screened out. When teachers use fallacies, they usually do so unconsciously and may not admit it, even when challenged by a quizzical youngster. A study of fallacies is of marginal value unless students have opportunities to appraise both good and bad thinking. Retention of understanding of fallacies requires that the knowledge be carried into other units and subject areas.

Deduction

A major part of the discipline of logic falls under the heading of deduction, which is defined as ". . . the application of a generalization to a specific instance, thereby reaching a conclusion."[4] The most common forms of deduction are the immediate inference, the syllogism, and the dilemma. Deduction contains simple elements but becomes immensely complex in the topics of truth functions and systems of symbolic logic.

Although students must have practice with deduction on the interpretation level starting in the early grades, it is a moot question as to how much should be attempted in the analysis category. In most instances, high-school courses dealing with logic omit a detailed consideration of deduction. In a personal experience in a teaching team, we attempted the instruction of conversion, obversion, and the categorical syllogism to heterogeneous classes of seniors in Problems of Democracy. Starting from the most elementary definitions of such terms as proposition, quantifier, subject term, connective, and predicate term, we progressed in six or seven class periods distributed through the first semester to the point where students were answering such questions as these:[5]

Directions: Write "yes" if the following statement is a proposition and "no" if it is not a proposition.

1. A. Some monopolies are legal.
   B. All corporations are included among those that pay a 52 percent tax on net income over $25,000.
2. A. No citizens are exempt from paying taxes.
   B. Pay your federal income tax by April 15.
3. A. Income taxes are a violation of the principle of the right to profit.
   B. Are income taxes constitutional?

Directions: Write on your paper the parts of the following proposition that are identified below.

Proposition: All bequeathed wealth is subject to inheritance taxes.

1. Connective

---

[4] James W. Johnson, *Logic and Rhetoric* (New York: Macmillan, 1962), p. 173.

[5] The questions on the next several pages will not be meaningful to a reader who has not studied deduction. The questions are included to illustrate how problems in formal deduction can be related to the social studies.

5. Quantifier
6. Term One
7. Term Two

Directions: Write the letter of the type of categorical proposition (A, E, I, O) that is illustrated in each of the following examples:

8. Some profits are not excessive.
9. Some profits are unreasonably high.
10. All businesses are not successful in earning profit.
11. All economic systems are included among those that answer the economic question.
12. Some government ownership of capital goods is found in modified capitalism.
13. All capitalistic nations are included among those that emphasize private ownership of consumer goods.
14. Some forms of competition are not ruthless.
15. Can the proposition in Question 8 be converted (conversion) to a reasonable conclusion?   (yes, no)
16. Can the proposition in Question 9 be converted (conversion) to a reasonable conclusion?   (yes, no)
17. Can the proposition in Question 10 be obverted (obversion) to a reasonable conclusion?   (yes, no)
18. Can the proposition in Question 11 be obverted (obversion) to a reasonable conclusion?   (yes, no)
19. Which letter represents the proper conversion of the following proposition?
    Proposition: Some competition is ruthless.
    A. All competition is ruthless.
    B. Some ruthless things are competition.
    C. Some competition is not ruthless.
    D. Some competition is ruthless.
20. Which letter represents the best obversion of the following proposition?
    Proposition: Some countries are capitalistic.
    A. Some countries are not capitalistic.
    B. All countries are not non-capitalistic.
    C. Some countries are not non-capitalistic.
    D. Some countries are capitalistic.
21. Is the first term in the proposition in Question 8 distributed or undistributed?

22. Is the first term in the proposition in Question 10 distributed or undistributed?
23. Is the second term in the proposition in Question 11 distributed or undistributed?
24. Is the second term in the proposition in Question 14 distributed or undistributed?

Directions: Identify the terms indicated after each of the following categorical syllogisms.

25. The Democratic Party is concerned with the welfare of the common man.
The Republican Party is not the Democratic Party.
The Republican Party is not concerned with the welfare of the common man.
Major term:
Minor term:

26. Some Republicans are not in favor of high taxes.
Some citizens of Wisconsin are not Republicans.
Some citizens of Wisconsin are in favor of high taxes.
Minor term:
Middle term:

27. All capitalists are believers in free enterprise.
Some socialists are not believers in free enterprise.
Some socialists are not capitalists.
Middle term:
Major term:

28. All illegal actions are against the public interest.
Some forms of monopoly are not against the public interest.
Some forms of monopoly are not illegal actions.
Minor Term:
Middle term:

29. Socialists are among those who say capitalism is planless and wasteful.
Mr. Smith says capitalism is planless and wasteful.
Mr. Smith is a socialist.
Major term:
Minor term:

Directions· Write the letter of the item listed below that applies to the syllogism.
   A. The syllogism contains the fallacy of four terms.
   B. The syllogism contains the fallacy of faulty exclusion.

    C. The syllogism contains the fallacy of the undistributed middle.

    D. The syllogism contains the fallacy of illicit distribution.

    E. The syllogism meets all rules and is valid.[6]

30. Which of the above letters applies to the syllogism in Question 25?

31. Which of the above letters applies to the syllogism in Question 26?

32. Which of the above letters applies to the syllogism in Question 27?

33. Which of the above letters applies to the syllogism in Question 28?

34. Which of the above letters applies to the syllogism in Question 29?

Directions: This syllogism is dedicated to all doubters. Can you find a fallacy?
Good things are among things that really exist.
Santa Claus is among good things.
Santa Claus is among things that really exist.

The vast majority of students learned to solve these problems, although some needed special help. The ideas were totally new to them and had a freshness that is not common in secondary-school social studies.

Our long-range plan for the study of deductive logic called for two more steps. The first was to present illustrations of deduction in their natural forms, such as in editorials or in parts of speeches. The students were to put the ideas in the argument into logical form and analyze them according to the rules for establishing validity and truth. The second step was to have students attempt deduction problems in all succeeding units through the year. We fell down on these two steps because we could not locate enough good examples of deduction in subject matter pertaining to our units, and, when we did encounter an example, the reasoning could usually be followed without putting the ideas into syllogistic form. Our experience does not warrant the conclusion that good examples of faulty and valid deductions do not exist;

[6] Winston Little, *Applied Logic* (Boston: Houghton Mifflin, 1955), p. 87.

but we were unable to find a sufficient number of them. With a dearth of good examples, we could not offer assignments in deduction often enough, so that students did not retain the definitions and processes learned at the beginning of the year; thus, a good deal of reteaching was necessary when we brought up deduction problems in later units. At this point, our team decided a strategic retreat was in order. We have not given up the hypothesis that some study of deduction is appropriate for the Problems of Democracy course; but we want more planning of the use of the process in all units before we attempt it again.

Semantics

Many important ideas from semantics are presented in English classes but are often ignored in the social studies or considered in such a haphazard manner that students miss their significance. Students should understand the symbolic nature of words that results in an arbitrary relationship between a word symbol and the entity to which it refers. One of the most difficult ideas to assimilate is the significance of the contradiction between two sets of ideas on word meaning—both of which are commonly accepted.

First set:
1. Words do not have a meaning that is logically implicit in their symbols.
2. Authors of dictionaries do not have authority to legislate what words are to mean. They write definitions on the basis of how they observe words to be used. Languages are constantly changing.
3. Speakers and writers have the right to stipulate the definition of a word that they use.

Second set:
1. Words are improperly used if they do not follow dictionary definitions.

2. Words are useless in communication unless a common meaning is assigned to them by the users.

The full understanding of this contradiction (treated here only superficially) leads to insight into the futile nature of arguments based on false assumptions about the meaning of words. Nothing is accomplished by arguing whether the United States is a republic or a democracy if the parties to the argument are defining the key terms differently and each insisting his definition is the right one. Because definitions play such an important part in every subject, students should learn the methods and standards for defining a word.

Pupils must become sensitive to the importance of the careful use of words in reasoning and communication. A recent economic report claimed that forty percent of the people in the United States live in poverty and deprivation. A student reading this report should immediately ask, "What does the author mean by 'poverty and deprivation'?" The answer in this case is that any family with an income of less than $4000 a year is living in poverty, and a family with less than $6000 income but more than $4000 a year lives in deprivation.

A proposed civil rights bill would apply to businesses that engage in a "substantial" amount of interstate commerce. A student's reaction should be that the word "substantial" does not have a sufficiently precise meaning to serve as a guide for the execution of a law.

Many words have an emotional, as well as intellectual, impact. Students recognize "socialism" and "communism" as "snarl words" but often cannot define the terms. The affective qualities of words and the resulting misuses should be understood.

Preparation for Analysis

Students should not be asked analysis questions until they have had special instruction in some phase of the parts and processes of reasoning. This original instruction falls in the memory, translation, and interpretation categories. For example, the deduction questions listed earlier in this chapter are best classified as interpretation, because, although they do deal with the parts and processes of reasoning, they are not asked in a true-to-life context. Examples of reasoning in everyday living do not appear as propositions set in syllogistic forms. The following exercises on "Causes and Conditions" and "The Meaning of Words" contain more examples of interpretation questions designed to prepare students for analysis in a senior course in Problems of Democracy. Both exercises are in the form of assignments for homework. Each starts with a description of some rules for reasoning and concludes with questions to give practice in using the rules.

Causes and Conditions:

Many nations look enviously at the riches of the United States. National leaders want their countries to become powerful and wealthy. They are interested in learning the secret of the success of the United States and want to know the "cause" of our success, so that they can duplicate it.

Logicians use the word "cause" in a special way which is useful. To understand their explanation of cause, it is necessary first to define the meaning of four kinds of conditions:

Necessary condition: A necessary condition is one without which a certain effect cannot occur. One logic book uses this example:

A certain kind of virus is a necessary condition of our having a . . . cold since it is presumably present in many persons all of the time, without their having colds.[7]

On the other hand, nobody gets a cold without having this virus. There are four possible relationships between a necessary condition (N) and a certain effect (E).

1. If N occurs, then E may or may not occur.
2. If N does not occur, then E cannot occur.

[7] Lionel Ruby, *Logic: An Introduction* (Chicago: Lippincott, 1960), p. 400.

3. If E occurs, then N must have occurred.
4. If E does not occur, then N may or may not have occurred.[8]

Sufficient condition: A sufficient condition is one that can produce a certain effect, but the same effect can be produced by other conditions. For example, the blowout of a tire is sufficient to bring about an accident, but other conditions can also produce an accident. There are four possible relationships between a sufficient condition and an effect.

1. If S occurs, then E occurs.
2. If S does not occur, then E may or may not occur.
3. If E occurs, then S may or may not have occurred.
4. If E does not occur, then S did not occur.

Necessary and sufficient condition: The logicians' meaning of cause is a combination of necessary and sufficient conditions. If necessary and sufficient conditions occur, then a certain effect will always occur and this effect will not occur without these conditions. Necessary and sufficient conditions are rare in life.

1. If NS occurs, then E will occur.
2. If NS does not occur, then E will not occur.
3. If E occurs, then NS has occurred.
4. If E does not occur, then NS has not occurred.

Contributory condition: It is often the case that a combination of conditions plays a part in bringing about an effect. This is particularly true in social studies. A number of contributory conditions can be necessary or sufficient conditions for an effect or a genuine cause.

Example:
It is widely believed that the following are among the factors that have an influence in bringing about a high income per capita in a nation:

A. the form of national economic system (capitalism, socialism, or communism);

[8] *Loc. cit.*

B. the form of government;
C. the amount of natural resources;
D. the level of education of the people;
E. the amount of industry and communication facilities.

Answer the following as true or false:

1. If capitalism is a necessary and sufficient cause for a wealthy nation, then nations wishing to become wealthy must adopt capitalism.
2. If capitalism is a sufficient condition for a wealthy nation, then a nation could become wealthy without adopting capitalism.
3. Capitalism, socialism, and communism might all be sufficient conditions for producing wealthy nations.
4. Capitalism, socialism, and communism might all be necessary conditions for a wealthy nation.
5. If a development of industry is a necessary and sufficient condition for a wealthy nation, then an agricultural nation without much industry cannot become wealthy.
6. If an educated population is a necessary condition for a wealthy nation, then a country that wants to become wealthy must invest money in education.
7. If a democratic government is a necessary contributory condition for a wealthy nation, then a dictatorship cannot be wealthy.

Nations are difficult to classify as to their economic systems, but some samples of nations in various stages of capitalism are the United States and Latin American countries. The Scandinavian nations and Northwestern Europe are considered to be socialistic. The only communist nations listed on the chart on pages 9–11 in your text are Czechoslovakia, USSR, Poland, and Hungary.[9] Using the information on the chart on pages 9–11, answer the following questions as true, false, or insufficient evidence.

8. Capitalism is a necessary condition for a high income per person. (Let us define a "high income per person" as above $500.)

[9] Baldwin Lee, *Capitalism and Other Economic Systems* (Washington, D. C.: Council for Advancement of Secondary Education, 1959), pp. 9–11.

9. Capitalism is a sufficient condition for a high income per person.
10. Capitalism is a necessary and sufficient condition for a high income per person.
11. Socialism is a necessary condition for a high income per person.
12. Socialism is a sufficient condition for a high income per person.
13. Socialism is a necessary and sufficient condition for a high income per person.
14. Communism is a necessary condition for a high income per person.
15. Communism is a sufficient condition for a high income per person.
16. Communism is a necessary and sufficient condition for a high income per person.

The Meaning of Words

Sometimes students are startled to read the statement: "The United States is not a democracy." This might be made by the communists because they define democracy only in terms of material security. They claim that their governments are more democratic, because the individual is guaranteed employment, medical care, housing, vacations, etc. In the United States we define democracy more in terms of freedom and popular sovereignty. We say that the communist countries are not democracies, because the people are denied freedom and an effective voice in government. Some loyal Americans say that the United States is not a democracy. These people state that a democracy is a system of government in which all people participate directly in making and administering the laws, such as in a New England town meeting. The people who offer this definition claim that the United States is a republic—that is, a system in which the elected representatives of the people make and execute the laws.

These definitions of democracy illustrate the fact that a word often is defined in a variety of ways. This causes difficulty in reasoning because logic requires a precise use of words and ideas. For example, look at this syllogism:

Major Premise: All democracies are in the Warsaw Pact.
Minor Premise: The United States is not in the Warsaw Pact.
Conclusion: The United States is not a democracy.

There is no question that this syllogism is valid, because it follows the rules; but most people in the United States would say that the conclusion is false as a result of a false major premise. However, people in Russia would claim that the syllogism is both valid and true. The real difference of opinion is caused by the difference in the definition of the word "democracy." Suppose, for sake of argument, that the citizens of the United States agree to the definition of democracy that the communists hold. Then we would say that the syllogism is both valid and true and would add that we are happy that the United States is not a democracy (communist style).

Do the communists have a right to change the meaning of democracy? After all, we established our meaning of the word first. The answer to this is that there are many words that have various and changing meanings. We have no right to expect other people to use these words exactly as we do. As a matter of fact, the word "democracy" has changed considerably in meaning in our own country. At the time our Constitution was written, many people used "democracy" to refer to the irresponsible rule of the mob.

The varied and changing definitions do not give us license to use words to mean anything we choose; we must use dictionary definitions. If we do use a word in a new or unusual manner, we should make certain that our readers or listeners understand our definition, and we should expect the same consideration from others.

In analyzing the truth and validity of a syllogism, the meaning of each word or phrase must be considered carefully to determine whether there is a possible difference of opinion on the definition that might have a bearing on the truth and validity of the syllogism. If you find such a term, you should state the definition you are using to make your judgment.

Directions: Underline the words or phrases in the following propositions that are indefinite in meaning. Write a brief statement after each indicating possible definitions that might be given to the word or phrase.

1. China is the largest nation on earth.
2. The Taft-Hartley Act is a slave-labor law.
3. Low tariffs are in the best interest of the United States.
4. Teenage marriages often end in divorce courts.
5. That which is good for the U.S. is good for the U.N.
6. Nuclear war would destroy civilization.

Examples of Analysis Questions

An analysis question by definition requires the solution of a problem in the light of conscious knowledge of the parts and processes of reasoning. As such, it must always be preceded by instruction in the form of reasoning required by the question. In all the following sample questions, the reader must assume that the student has had the instruction necessary to answer them. Question 1 is based on induction. Notice that the question does not mention induction, because the student is expected to ascertain that this process is the one involved. Question 2 is based on fallacies and semantics. Question 5 tests the student's ability to recognize argument by analogy and to know the limitations of this form of reasoning. Question 6 asks the student to use the knowledge on "causes and conditions" that is offered earlier in this chapter.

1. A political inventory was sent to 250 members of the Democratic Party and to an equal number of members of the Republican Party in Manitowoc County. What conclusions concerning the beliefs of the members of the two parties do you believe are justified from the following information?

Political Inventory: Indicate whether you believe each of the following statements about government is "generally true" or "generally false":

A. "That government is best which governs least."
Results: Republican Male: True 47   False 12
         Republican Female: True 22   False 6
         Democratic Male: True 15   False 30
         Democratic Female: True 5   False 18

B. "Centralization is bad; decentralization is good."
Results: Republican Male: True 43   False 10
         Republican Female: True 19   False 6
         Democratic Male: True 17   False 26
         Democratic Female: True 6   False 12

C. "The national government has greatly encroached upon the powers and activities of state and local governments."
Results: Republican Male: True 50   False 8
         Republican Female: True 21   False 5
         Democratic Male: True 15   False 29
         Democratic Female: True 3   False 17

D. "Every law which is enacted reduces individual freedom."
Results: Republican Male: True 20   False 39
         Republican Female: True 13   False 15
         Democratic Male: True 7   False 37
         Democratic Female: True 3   False 20

E. "Economic growth can be stimulated by reducing government spending and relying on the resourcefulness of the American people to enlarge the economy."
Results: Republican Male: True 48   False 8
         Republican Female: True 23   False 2
         Democratic Male: True 11   False 29
         Democratic Female: True 4   False 18

F. "Economic growth can best be stimulated by a tax cut; but any great reduction in government spending would have a harmful effect on the economy."
Results: Republican Male: True 21   False 34
         Republican Female: True 8   False 18
         Democratic Male: True 31   False 8
         Democratic Female: True 20   False 3

G. "Government on the local, state, and national level owns too much property and operates too many businesses in competition with private enterprise."

Results: Republican Male: True 42 False 16
          Republican Female: True 19 False 8
          Democratic Male: True 7   False 37
          Democratic Female: True 4   False 20

H. "There is no real difference in principle between the Democratic and Republican parties because both include the whole range from liberal to conservative."

Results: Republican Male: True 15 False 43
          Republican Female: True 8   False 20
          Democratic Male: True 14 False 24
          Democratic Female: True 8   False 16

2. Analyze the reasoning in these statements overheard recently:
   A. I will not have anything to do with the march to Washington designed to call attention to problems of discrimination against minorities, because the Negro who is organizing the demonstration has been convicted of several crimes.
   B. The League of Women Voters claims to be nonpartisan in politics, but it demonstrated the falsity of this claim by taking a position on the state sales tax issue.
   C. Labor unions cannot be considered to hold a monopoly, because less than one out of three members of the civilian work force belong to a union.

3. Analyze the reasoning in this quotation from a speech by Khrushchev:
   "At our previous meeting, Comrade Yevtushenko spoke in defense of abstractionism [in art]. He tried to justify this position by arguing that there are good men among both realists and formalists, and he referred in this connection to two German painters who disagreed sharply about art but later died in the same trench fighting for the revolution. Such a fact may have occurred in life as an individual case. However, one can quote an example of quite a different character. After the Civil War, an ugly formalist memorial was erected in the town of Artemovsk in the Ukraine. Its author was the cubist sculptor Kavaleridze. It was a horrible sight, although the cubists admired it. During the war, the memorial was destroyed. The sculptor of this formalist memorial, remaining on territory

'Twas ever thus

—Cleveland Plain Dealer

occupied by the fascists, behaved in an unworthy manner. Thus the example quoted by Comrade Yevtushenko cannot serve as a serious argument in support of his views."[10]

4. Analyze the reasoning in the above cartoon.[11]

5. Analyze the reasoning in these statements:
   A. Every thirty years the United States has had a depression. The last depression was about thirty years ago, so we can expect another at any time.
   B. If world government is not adopted, there will be a nuclear

[10] *NATO Letter*, July/August, 1963, p. 24.
[11] *Milwaukee Journal*, July 14, 1963, part 5, p. 3. (Reprint of cartoon by Edward Kuekes in *Cleveland Plain Dealer*.)

war that will destroy civilization. Man must not be allowed to destroy himself.

C. The Republican Party caused the depression of the 1930s, because it was in control of the federal government when the depression started.

6. Analyze the reasoning in the following quotation:

"In our climate of freedom in which we live, we outproduce every other country in the world.

"Take Soviet Russia, for instance: In size, Russia is twice as large as the United States.

"In population, Russia has one-fifth more people than the United States.

"Russia has an abundance of natural resources.

"But in the actual production of goods and services—and this includes *both capital goods and consumer goods*—we in this country, in our climate of freedom, outproduce Soviet Russia more than two to one."[12]

The Uses of Analysis Questions

Potentially, analysis is one of the most important categories of thinking, but much planning and experimentation is necessary to bring it to fruition. An effort is made in this chapter to suggest possible points of attack; teachers may see opportunities to develop certain aspects of reasoning in their current units. Examples of inductive reasoning are common in elementary school texts, and teachers can profitably offer simple instruction and practice in the process. Above all, elementary teachers can stress the fact that conclusions must follow the evidence. A sixth- or seventh-grade unit on the Soviet Union provides an ideal opportunity to investigate propaganda techniques. In junior high school, students are usually introduced to the scientific method. Social studies teachers can profitably bring up the study of methodology in their field and show how it compares to that in science.

Full use of analysis will require enterprising school systems to

[12] Arch N. Booth, "Making Self-Government Work," *Vital Speeches,* July 15, 1963, p. 606.

engage in broad study and experimentation in all grades and subjects to determine a practical sequence for the instruction of reasoning. This need not unduly upset the curricular pattern, as the study of reasoning can be superimposed on the subject matter already defined for each grade and subject. This project could bring about a dramatic advance in the quality of reasoning.

• • •

The following books are recommended as excellent sources of information for teachers who have never formally studied reasoning or who feel the need of refreshing their knowledge on the subject:

Brennan, Joseph Gerard, *A Handbook of Logic* (New York: Harper & Row, 1961).

Black, Max *Critical Thinking* (Englewood Cliffs, N.J.: Prentice-Hall, 1952).

Chase, Stuart, *Guides to Straight Thinking* (New York: Harper & Row, 1956).

Graves, Harold F., and Oldsey, Bernard S., *From Fact to Judgement* (New York: Macmillan, 1963).

Hayakawa, S. I., *Language in Thought and Action* (New York: Harcourt, Brace & World, 1949).

Johnson, James William, *Logic and Rhetoric* (New York: Macmillan, 1962).

Little, Wilson, and Moore, W. Edgar, *Applied Logic* (Boston: Houghton Mifflin, 1955).[13]

Ruby, Lionel *Logic* (Chicago: Lippincott, 1960).[13]

Werkmeister, W. H., *An Introduction to Critical Thinking* (Lincoln, Neb.: Johnsen Publishing Company, 1957).[13]

QUESTIONS ON CHAPTER SIX

1.____ True or False: One reason many teachers may have difficulty in using the analysis category is that they lack special preparation for this type of thinking.

2.____ True or False: Teachers who have not studied formal thinking can prepare themselves to use the analysis category by studying one or more references listed at the end of this chapter.

[13] These books are especially recommended.

3._____ True or False: Before students are asked to answer analysis questions, they should have instruction on certain phases of formal thinking.

4._____ True or False: In the analysis category, a student who answers a question requiring the use of the thought process of extrapolation need not be conscious of the fact that he is engaging in extrapolation.

5._____ A student comments that the United Nations should be strengthened by changing it from a confederation to a federation. To support his contention, he points out that our country was divided and weak under the Articles of Confederation but became united and strong under a federal Constitution. The teacher asks for comment on the argument. Which of the following responses is on the analysis level?

    A. "The argument offers an analogy from the early history of our nation to prove the need for centralizing the power of the United Nations. An analogy often provides a fruitful source of hypotheses but never can be considered to be proof. A weakness of this analogy is that the relations among the thirteen original colonies are quite different from those among modern nations."

    B. "Just because a federation was more suitable for the thirteen original states does not necessarily mean that a federation would be best for the nations of the world. The people in the thirteen states had similar political, economic, cultural, and religious institutions. The nations of the world today are made up of people who have far less in common."

6._____ True or False: A student who answers a question successfully on the analysis level might not be able to answer it on the interpretive level.

7._____ True or False: A student who successfully answers a question on the interpretation level might not be able to answer it on the analysis level.

8._____ True or False: A question should not be presented to a class if there is doubt as to whether it is classified as interpretation or as analysis.

9._____ Which of the following are recommended in this chapter for experimental study on the analysis level in elementary school? (A) Semantics; (B) Induction; (C) Deduction; (D) Fallacy.

10._____ The definition of analysis presented in this chapter differs somewhat from that given in a dictionary. This illustrates a problem in: (A) Semantics; (B) Induction; (C) Deduction; (D) Fallacy.

11._____ An analysis question in which the student is expected to put an example of thinking into the form of a syllogism illustrates a problem in: (A) Semantics; (B) Induction; (C) Deduction; (D) Fallacy.

12._____ A teacher who studied the taxonomy of questions decided to gather evidence on the kinds of questions asked of students. He visited the classes of five teachers and concluded that in general teachers ask eight times as many memory questions as they do above-memory questions. From the evidence given, which of the standards for good induction was most clearly violated? (A) The criterion of the number of instances; (B) No contrary instances; (C) Nonvariable character of the phenomenon under investigation; (D) Independent confirmation by deduction from more general laws.

13. Which of the following cause and effect relations *do you believe* exists between the study of the taxonomy of questions by a teacher (the condition) and the increased skill in asking classroom questions (the effect)? Justify your answer in two or three sentences.

A. The study of the taxonomy of questions is a *necessary* condition for increased skill in questioning.

B. The study of the taxonomy of questions is a *sufficient condition* for increased skill in questioning.

C. The study of the taxonomy of questions is a *necessary and sufficient condition* for increased skill in questioning.

RELATING THE TAXONOMY OF QUESTIONS TO A UNIT
OF YOUR CHOICE

14. Write your own list of characteristics of analysis questions to serve as a reference.

15. Choose for further study a topic from formal logic that is introduced in this chapter. Decide whether analysis questions using this logical process would be appropriate for your unit. If so, write several analysis questions.

ANSWERS TO QUESTIONS ON
CHAPTER SIX

1. True.
2. True.
3. True.
4. False.
5. A.
6. False.
7. True.
8. False.
9. B.
10. A.
11. C.
12. A.
13. The words "do you believe" in the question indicate that the
answer is somewhat subjective. My choice of an answer is B.
There are other ways of increasing skill in questioning, so the
condition cannot be called necessary. Not every teacher who
studies the taxonomy will increase skill in questioning. Some
may prefer to emphasize other goals than the cognitive and
others may not understand the tool well enough to use it.
However, this book is based on the hypothesis that the study
of questions can increase skill in their use. Experimentation
may prove this to be a sufficient condition to bring about the
desired effect.

SEVEN

❖

SYNTHESIS

Introduction

SYNTHESIS QUESTIONS encourage students to engage in imaginative, original thinking. Some teachers argue that creativity is too advanced a process to be practiced by students. These teachers are thinking of creativity as illustrated by the accomplishments of men like Euclid, Leonardo da Vinci, Beethoven, John Locke, and Jonas Salk. They were truly creative on the ultimate level, but the same thought processes in an elementary form can be practiced by students. Instead of pushing back the frontier of human knowledge, students can discover knowledge that is *new to them*. They can deal with simple problems that require creative answers rather than undertake the most complex and important problems that face man.

125

Creativity in any field requires certain skills, but, more than that, it requires a certain temperament and personality. The creative person has a questioning mind—a sensitivity to problems. He is a bit of a renegade with a restless disposition that "cannot leave well enough alone." He cannot accept any dogma as being so well established that it is beyond doubting and questioning. A high fluency of ideas, including novel ones, is another sign of creativity. A creative person has a flexibility that makes possible dramatic conceptual changes, but he is not a scatterbrain flitting haphazardly from idea to idea. He has a sound conceptual organization of his field and an ability to translate, interpret, apply, analyze, and evaluate, as well as synthesize. He has a tenacity of purpose that makes it possible to overcome the inevitable frustration involved in the process of discovery. Philip Jackson and Jacob Getzels in their study of creativity at the University of Chicago note that many students with high intelligence quotients tend to seek the "safe" answer to a question.[1] These students accept the idea that the teacher and the textbook can be relied upon as the guide to learning. The creative student glories in discovering a different answer that can be logically or artistically justified.

Synthesis thinking is not so closely tied to the form of the questions as is true in other categories but instead is fostered by a classroom atmosphere that seeks and rewards originality. In the definition of almost every previous category, it was noted that students may demonstrate creative thinking by figuring out an accurate and sometimes ingenious answer that the teacher does not anticipate. On the other hand, teachers frequently present problems particularly designed to stimulate original thinking and get only the most obvious, stereotyped answers.

What are the characteristics of synthesis questions? First, these questions allow students great freedom in seeking solutions. Most questions in previous categories limit students to subject matter and thought processes that are stated or implicit in the question, while restrictions of this type are kept at a minimum in the

[1] *Christian Science Monitor*, December 12, 1960, p. 6.

synthesis category. In addition, the questions are of the type that have many possible approaches. Thus, the student is encouraged to use information and thought processes he may know about from any part of his life experience. He must understand that the teacher does not have in mind a definite answer which he is expected to duplicate.[2]

Another explanation of the freedom involved in synthesis is the distinction between convergent and divergent thinking. In convergent thinking, the course of thought starts with a problem that offers a variety of apparent possibilities and converges to *one* correct answer. Synthesis calls for divergent thinking, which starts from a problem that offers a variety of possibilities radiating out to *many* satisfactory answers. Following are samples of questions developed at the University of Wisconsin for an experimental test designed to measure creativity. Although these particular questions have no practical use in the social studies, they do illustrate the nature of divergent thinking:

Directions: In this test you are to read a story and then write *as many* interesting titles for it as you can. You will have two minutes.

A young missionary is caught by a tribe of wild savages. He is put in a large pot and is about to be boiled. Suddenly a beautiful young girl, a princess of the tribe, offers to save him if he will become her husband. The missionary refuses and is boiled to death.

Directions: Suppose that you decide to manufacture a *regular wood pencil* that will sell better than any other. List the problems

---

[2] In a previous chapter this statement was made: "Application questions include a minimum of directions or instructions." This sounds much like the need for "freedom" in a synthesis question. However, there is a distinct difference of emphasis. Directions are kept at a minimum in application questions, because the student is expected to know what to do as a result of previous instruction. There is usually one right way to solve an application problem and the student is expected to demonstrate it. On a synthesis question, the lack of specific directions results from the fact that there are many ways to solve the problem.

you would work on in order to *make* a better pencil. You will have three minutes to list as many problems as you can.

A second characteristic of questions in the synthesis category is that the solution requires a product. In Bloom's *Taxonomy of Educational Objectives,* the authors define three kinds of products:

1. "Production of a unique communication"
The student conveys an idea which is designed to inform, convince, or entertain.
2. "Production of a plan, or proposed set of operations"
A problem is presented that offers numerous possible approaches. The student must devise a new procedure to solve the problem.
3. "Derivation of a set of abstract relations"[3]
This may be performed as inductive or deductive thinking. In the former case, a mass of related information is presented to the student, and he is asked to find a pattern. In the latter, he is given one or more generalizations and asked to produce a new idea. Although a synthesis question always requires a product, it does not follow that any question asking for a product automatically falls in the synthesis category. For instance, essay questions frequently emphasize only memory, and translation questions may require students to draw pictures or portray written information. The true synthesis question permits more freedom of expression.

There are weaknesses of synthesis questions that must be noted. One is the possibility of asking questions similar to puzzles in that they call for mental gymnastics but have no significance. The question asking the student to write titles for the story about the missionary being boiled to death is an example of a synthesis question having no real significance. Social studies are filled with genuine problems demanding creative thought; so there is no need to deal with trivia.

[3] Benjamin S. Bloom (ed.), *Taxonomy of Educational Objectives* (New York: Longmans, Green, 1956), pp. 168–172.

Another potential weakness of synthesis is the possibility of forming questions that are totally beyond the competency of the student. The right to attempt to be creative demands some knowledge of the situation. By his years of study, MacKinlay Kantor won the right to speculate creatively on how American history would have been different if the South had been victorious in the Civil War. The argument that students must have some competency before attempting to be creative can be carried to the point where students have no right to be creative on any complex subject. The teacher must find a middle position in which creative questions are not answered by wild imagination but by creative speculation on topics in which students have less than full competency.

The biggest weakness of synthesis questions is the difficulty in evaluating the answers fairly. One of the writer's students complained, "You tell us to be original in our thinking, but every time I get off the beaten track you give me a low mark." This caused me to speculate on whether I was correct in evaluating his originality as being of low quality or whether I just didn't recognize ingenuity when I saw it. A teacher is tempted to avoid synthesis questions or to ignore them in grading. These are irresponsible evasions. Suggestions are offered in Chapter Nine on ways to minimize difficulties in evaluating synthesis answers.

Examples of Synthesis Questions

1. In an earlier chapter the research paper was described as a good problem on the application level. However, it can reach a high level of excellence in application and still not be very original. A wag commented that stealing ideas from a single book is plagiarism but copying ideas from many books is research. Too often this is the case in student research. A written or oral report can challenge students to be creative if the teacher makes the proper preparations. First he must make certain that the students

understand the meaning of original thinking. The following ideas should be presented:

A. Progress in the world comes through original thinking.
B. To be creative in making a report, students must make the information more meaningful, more understandable, or more useful as a result of it passing through their minds.
C. Originality may result from using ingenious sources of information; from organizing ideas in a new and better way; or from discovering a new relationship or a new conclusion.
D. To be original in a report means to shed new light on a subject. However, everything new is not necessarily good. An artist may paint a picture wholly different from anything painted before, but it may be hideous. An original report must not only be a *new* way to look at a topic, but a *better* way.
E. Creativity is usually accompanied by many false starts and considerable frustration. A person who gives up easily is unlikely to be creative.

Second, in order to encourage creative thinking, a teacher can assign report topics that offer opportunities for originality. Some topics almost force creativity, while others stifle it. Following are suggestions for identifying good topics:

A. Subjects in which a student can discover raw, undigested information offer opportunities for originality. Local history is good, because the pupil can dig into newspapers, family records, city records, industrial records, and church records. Chances are that historians and other social scientists have never seen these sources. Therefore, any conclusions drawn that accurately explain or summarize the facts are likely to be original. Subjects on which information has been available for a long time and sifted by many minds are so well digested as not to offer much opportunity for originality. It is difficult to do original thinking with information from textbooks, encyclopedias, and other similar sources that are highly refined summaries.

B. Originality is often encouraged by defining a topic as a problem on which there is genuine doubt as to the best explanation or solution. On such a topic, the student can examine all sides and give his personal conclusion. The best controversial issues to stimulate original thinking are not the old standards which are argued in schools every year, such as: *Should capital punishment be abolished?* or *Should eighteen-year-olds have the right to vote?* On issues like these, students can easily find ready-made arguments on either side.

C. Relating a general problem to a local situation often makes originality possible. For instance, instead of writing about the St. Lawrence Seaway, the student might be asked to discuss the subject: *What the St. Lawrence Seaway Means to Our Community.* A similar type of question would be: *Is There a Need for a Junior College in Our Community?* The subject relates a general problem to a specific case.

D. For more mature students, an original term paper can be composed on the basis of a study of the writings of an author or of the publications of an organization. For example, after reading the fictional writings of an author, they can draw generalizations about his style, beliefs, and personality.

E. An incomplete story in current events, such as the Berlin stalemate or international disarmament, presents an opportunity for originality by letting students review the issue and make their own predictions and recommendations.

2. One product of synthesis is the "derivation of a set of abstract relations." An opportunity for this type of thinking comes up in a labor-management unit for seniors in high school. In many recent strikes the most prickly issues are not wages and hours, but the fact that labor wants to enter into decisions in other areas and management balks. The next exercise is an effort to determine whether it is possible to set up standards that might be useful in solving these disputes. The form of the problem requiring most creativity would be: *Devise a set of principles or standards that would be helpful in defining the proper division of*

decision power between labor and management. This is a good synthesis problem because it is real and because the sky is the limit for ingenious creative thought. However, students who are less creative or less motivated would find it difficult to get a foothold. To get them started, the following list of questions involving production is presented:

Directions: Which in this list do you believe are legitimate questions for collective bargaining?

A. How much should workers of various skills be paid?
B. How much should managers be paid?
C. How much vacation should workers have?
D. How fast should the assembly line move?
E. Is a particular worker incompetent and deserving of being discharged?
F. For what price should the products be offered for sale?
G. Who should be selected as officers of a company?
H. Should a new plant be constructed to expand production?
I. How much should be paid the owners of the company in dividends?
J. What new products should be produced?
K. How many laborers are required to do a certain job?
L. To what extent should automation be introduced into the factory?
M. From whom should raw materials and other necessary products be purchased?
N. How much should be spent on advertising?
O. How much should be spent on research?
P. Which men should be laid off first?
Q. Should workers have rest periods?
R. Should employers pay for sickness and retirement benefits?

These questions are helpful as some are obviously to be answered exclusively by management, while others are clearly legitimate for collective bargaining, and the rest have a doubtful status. After studying this list, students are presented with this synthesis problem: *What principles or standards can you devise that would be helpful in determining which of the above questions should be decided by collective bargaining?* This could be presented for individual study, although the following ideas resulted from discussion in class:

A. Workers should have the right to bargain on questions that immediately and directily affect wages, hours, and working conditions. Current law gives them this right.

B. Managers should make decisions in which there is little or no conflict of interests with workers.

C. Manager and workers should participate in those decisions in which they have a special competency that the other side does not possess or possesses to a lesser degree.

D. A principle of capitalism gives owners a right to initiate and operate a business. Under laissez-faire capitalism this right was almost absolute, but it has been limited to an indefinite degree.

3. This is an exercise asking eighth-grade students to derive a set of abstract relations in a unit on the Civil War. As an introductory step, the students identify the most important and the least important questions for historical study from the following list:

A. What were the causes of the Civil War?

B. Could the Civil War have been prevented if the leaders had made wiser decisions?

C. Were the slaves of the South better off than factory workers in the North?

D. Was Jefferson Davis a capable leader?

E. Is slavery wrong?

F. Which side won the Battle of Gettysburg?

G. What was the population of New Orleans in 1861?

H. If Grant had been in command of the Northern armies from the beginning of the Civil War, would it have been concluded sooner?

I. What were the results of the Civil War?

J. Who was President of the United States during the Civil War?

K. What were the strengths and weaknesses of the North and South as they entered the Civil War?

Next, the students are asked: *What are the qualities of a question that make it important for historical study? What are the qualities of a question that make it unimporant for historical study?*
The teacher should allow several minutes for thought before permitting anyone to volunteer an answer. Another approach is to require a written answer, as this will force every student to attack the problem. When done orally, some depend on the few quick-minded and articulate students to answer all difficult questions.

4. The ability to ask the right questions when faced by a problem calls for a kind of creativity illustrated in the following examples:

A. A band of pioneers is pushing into the American frontier area searching for a site to settle. Two scouts are sent out in different directions to find favorable locations. Both report that they have located excellent places. What questions would you ask the scouts to determine which has found the better location?

B. A student is assigned to make a report in class the next day. He finds a number of books in the library that deal with the specified topic but has only time to get the necessary information from one of them. What questions would he ask about the books to help him choose the best one?

5. The formation of plausible hypotheses is an important phase of the problem-solving process. Students first need instruction on the nature and function of hypotheses. Then the skill is developed through the use of questions, such as the following, which would come early in a unit:

A. What hypotheses can you suggest that would explain why nations in the tropics seldom develop a high level of civilization?

B. What hypotheses can you suggest that would explain why the political party that gains control of Congress in a presidential election year almost always loses seats in the mid-term elections?

C. How many hypotheses can you suggest that would explain why Mao Tse-tung did not attend the May Day celebrations in China in 1963?

This kind of synthesis question tempts some students to give humorous answers. For example, Question 5C above was originally composed by a teacher after reading editorial speculation on the matter. Mao Tse-tung's absence from the May Day celebrations could have significance in international affairs; however, the class clown can almost be counted upon to come up with the explanation that Mao might have fallen off his monolith or have had an acute case of hiccups. Even this form of originality deserves a smile but should be followed by a reminder that the question deserves serious consideration.

6. Speculation on possible courses of action in a particular situation can challenge the imagination.

A. What are the possible courses of action that the United States might take regarding the menace of communism in Cuba?

B. What are the possible courses of action that our community might use to attract new industries?

C. Suggest ways that the United States might get spies into the Soviet Union.

D. What are possible courses of action Lincoln might have taken when he learned that Fort Sumter had been attacked?

7. Students can be asked to *plan* appropriate courses of action. These projects resemble some described in the application category, but they certainly offer opportunities for creativity.

A. Draw up a plan that our class could follow to bring pressure on the legislature to pass a law to _____.

B. Draw up a plan for the observance of United Nations Day.

C. Write a constitution appropriate for the Student Council.

D. Draw up a plan in which the class could participate in the campaign to make the election of the President of the United States dependent on popular vote.

8. The designing of a simple experiment calls for creativity. In some cases the teacher may want the experiments carried out, while in others he may simply wish the students to have the experience in planning them. If the latter is true, students may assume that plenty of money and time are available to do whatever they feel necessary to solve the problem.

A. Devise a plan to determine whether the Democrats and Republicans are evenly distributed throughout the city, or whether the supporters of each party are concentrated in certain wards.

B. Devise a plan to determine whether national ancestry of students in our school is related to intelligence.

C. Devise a plan to determine whether students who salute the flag each day in school are more patriotic than those who do not have this experience.[4]

A Spirit of Creativity in the Classroom

Cultivating creative thinking requires more than asking questions in the synthesis category. Most important is the development of a classroom atmosphere that encourages divergent thought. The teacher and class should respect unusual answers and questions. Respect can be shown for original ideas by listening to them, discussing them, testing them, communicating them to appropriate individuals or groups, and by giving credit for them.[5] A teacher with a well-organized pattern of subject matter

[4] Questions similar to these are found in the analysis category, but the emphasis here is on creative imagination rather than on the logic of experimental procedures. A student can know the latter and still not be good at this kind of problem unless he has a creative imagination.

[5] E. Paul Torrance, *Education and the Creative Potential* (Minneapolis: University of Minnesota Press, 1963), pp. 56–58.

and plan of action in his mind must resist the temptation to brush aside student ideas that do not fit easily into his plan.

A classroom atmosphere conducive to original thinking is not one in which the teacher refuses to take responsibility for orderly instruction that moves toward a goal. Many ideas or questions asked by students are faulty or irrelevant in some way and should be identified as such by the teacher. However, the spirit in which this is done should encourage students to try again. The teacher says in effect, "This appears to me to be the weakness in your idea. Do you agree? Good for you for trying and better luck next time."

A teacher must have certain personality characteristics to be successful in encouraging creativity. An insecure teacher who uses his position of authority to bolster his ego is not likely to welcome the challenges posed by creative thinking. He is apt to interpret the creative student's questioning, doubting, and challenging as insubordination. A teacher must be able to gain satisfaction from a new idea created by one of his students.

QUESTIONS ON CHAPTER SEVEN

1._____ Which of the following is *not* a characteristic of synthesis questions? (A) There is not one correct answer to the question but rather many possible answers. (B) The question allows more freedom in seeking an answer than in other lower categories. (C) In answering the question, the student creates a product or communication. (D) The question leads to a response which can only be subjectively evaluated by a teacher. (E) All of the above are characteristics of synthesis questions.

2._____ Which attitude on the part of a teacher is likely to produce more synthesis questions in a classroom?
   A. The subject I teach offers important knowledge that must be communicated to my students. For students to understand this knowledge they must be able to remember and apply it.
   B. The subject I teach offers important knowledge that students must remember and use. The subject also

offers problems as yet unsolved and opportunities for refinement and reinterpretation with which my students and I can grapple.

3.____ A student reasons out a mathematical procedure to solve a problem. He shows it to his teacher and is told that he has discovered a procedure that mathematicians have long used. Should the student's discovery be considered creative? (Answer "yes" or "no".)

4.___ True or False: Synthesis questions are appropriate for junior and senior high school but not for elementary school.

5.____ True or False: A synthesis question guarantees an ingenious answer.

6.___ True or False: A question that is properly classified in a category below synthesis may stimulate a student to creative thinking.

7.____ True or False: It is possible for a person to be highly intelligent as measured by scholastic aptitude tests and still be low in creativity.

8.___ True or False: It is possible for a person to be high in intelligence and high in creativity.

9.___ Decide whether each statement best describes application or synthesis categories:

____A. Specific, detailed directions are not offered in this category of questions because the student is expected to know from previous learning what is required to solve the problem.

____B. Specific, detailed directions are not offered in this category of questions because there are many correct approaches.

10. Classify each of the following questions as memory, translation, interpretation, application, analysis or synthesis:

____A. Write a synthesis question based on the subject matter in this chapter.

____B. Compare application thinking with interpretation thinking.

____C. Write a summary of this chapter.

____D. What are the two main characteristics of synthesis questions?

____E. Draw a symbolic representation of convergent and divergent thinking.

11. A man who judges many art shows commented that 75 percent of the time the judges agree on the pictures that show merit but that occasionally their decisions are widely different. What significance does this statement have to teachers who are interested in synthesis questions? (Write one or two sentences.)

12. In addition to asking synthesis questions, what can a teacher do to encourage creative thinking in his classroom?

RELATING THE TAXONOMY OF QUESTIONS TO A UNIT
OF YOUR CHOICE

13. Write your own list of characteristics of synthesis questions to serve as a reference.

14. Write five or more synthesis questions.

ANSWERS TO QUESTIONS ON
CHAPTER SEVEN

1. E.
2. B.   Sometimes teachers forget that all subject disciplines are in a state of growth. Students should be encouraged to grapple with problems on the frontiers of knowledge. They are not likely to revolutionize the subject, but they can learn much by this kind of thinking.
3. Yes.
4. False.
5. False.
6. True.   One of the best ways to foster creative thinking is to recognize and encourage it whenever it appears.
7. True.
8. True.
9. A. Application;   B. Synthesis.
10. A. Interpretation (Specification of both the kind of question and the general subject matter of the question points toward interpretation. However, the divergent possibilities for responses suggests that an answer of "synthesis" could be justified.);   B. Interpretation;   C. Translation;   D. Memory of translation,   E. Translation. (This is the kind of question in which the teacher may seek a simple translated answer but often finds that the student goes into interpretation or even synthesis.)

11. The evaluation of answers in the synthesis category is a subjective process similar to judging the quality of pictures. This evaluation of the products of synthesis is difficult but necessary in order to give students practice in creative thinking.
12. Ingenious ideas devised by students should be praised and used and rewarded in the grading system. Faulty efforts to be creative should be treated tolerantly in order to encourage students to try again.

EIGHT

❖

EVALUATION

Definition of Evaluation

ANY IDEA OR OBJECT can be evaluated in two main steps. The first is to set up appropriate standards or values and the second is to determine how closely the idea or object meets these standards or values. A relatively simple form of evaluation is observed in the services of organizations, such as the Consumers Union, which tests and rates consumer goods as a guide for buyers. An article in *Consumer Reports* presented a summary of the evaluation of eighteen models of room air-conditioning units [1] The first step was to determine the qualities of a good room air-conditioner and

[1] "Room Air Conditioners," *Consumer Reports*, June, 1963, pp. 284–291.

these seven main standards were identified and defined: dehumidification, temperature uniformity, average cycling spread, condensate disposal, cooling under extreme conditions, relative noise level inside, and relative noise level outside. Each model was judged on every standard as being excellent, very good, good, fairly good, fair, or poor. On the basis of these evaluations, two models were recommended as being "acceptable." This example of evaluation illustrates the two main steps and results in a clearcut conclusion. Unfortunately, the process of evaluation is usually not so simple. The values in judging a room air-conditioner are fairly obvious and noncontroversial, and the measure of each model against the values can be made with almost mathematical precision. In contrast, many values commonly used in the social studies are controversial and have an abstract quality making them loose standards for measurement.

To qualify in this category, a question must require the student to perform both steps in evaluation. If no standards are offered in the question or if the standards are only suggestive and require refinement in order to perform the second step, then the question is classified as evaluation. Questions that specify the values for use in making a judgment may be good intellectual exercises, but they are better classified as interpretation. This is an arbitrary part of the definition necessary to distinguish the thinking from other categories.

A hazy dividing line exists between evaluation and interpretation. This is illustrated in a teacher's thinking when he corrects an objective test. On each question, the teacher compares the student's response to the correct answer. If a memory question asks for the name of the first President of the United States and the student writes "Jefferson," the answer is wrong. If the interpretation question asks for the latitude of Cairo, and the student writes "30° North," the answer is right. In a sense, the teacher follows the two steps of evaluation, because he sets a standard (the correct answer) and judges accordingly. However, the thinking of the teacher can better be explained under the definition of interpretation. He finds the relationship between a correct, objective answer and the student's response. An advantage of classifying this kind of objective judgment as interpretation is that it reserves the much more difficult problem of subjective judgment for the evaluation category.

Evaluation is always somewhat subjective in one of two ways. Either the standard cannot be proven to be correct, or the idea to be judged cannot be proven to violate or illustrate the standard. This difference in the thinking required to correct objective and subjective answers is apparent to any teacher. The latter kind of thinking deserves special study and practice by students.

Preparing Students to Evaluate

Evaluation questions are easy to compose and are frequently used in class discussion, although often the experience amounts to a heated exchange of ignorance. This is caused by the students' lack of understanding of the rules for this form of thinking. Like analysis, the process of evaluation requires preparatory instruction, which falls mainly in the memory and interpretation categories.

Skill in evaluation requires knowledge of the nature of values. One logician offers this definition: "By 'values' we refer to objects or situations or activities which are liked, or desired, or approved by human beings."[2] Facts can be determined to be true or false, but values cannot. We endorse democratic values in this nation, although neither inductive nor deductive logic can *prove* that they are best.

The source and nature of values are subject to philosophic controversy. Perhaps the most common interpretation is that there are standards for right and wrong that are a part of nature. These standards are sometimes related to a religion or to an interpreta-

[2] Lionel Ruby, *Logic* (Chicago: Lippincott, 1960), p. 473.

tion of history, such as dialectical materialism. In the Declaration of Independence, there is a famous statement of values:

We hold these truths to be self-evident; that all men are created equal; that they are endowed by their Creator with certain unalienable rights; that among these are life, liberty, and the pursuit of happiness.

The authors conceive this to be a law of nature that is correct for all places and all times.

A second theory relates values to a particular culture. Evidence from anthropology shows the extreme diversity of human values among the peoples of the world. Some scholars conclude there are no standards of values that apply to all times and places. Rather, the definitions of right and wrong or good and bad are whatever the social group determines them to be. Anthropologists point out that values of a culture are not purely products of human caprice but reflect the needs of the people. For example, a primitive hunting economy seldom provides for polygamous marriage, because wives and children are of little economic assistance to a hunter. On the other hand, women and children play a necessary role in a herding economy, and this form of enterprise is frequently associated with polygamous marriage. Those who relate values to culture claim that, although we condemn polygamy as immoral, the practice is not necessarily wrong for people in other cultures. We should judge other people according to their values —not according to ours.

The third general theory of value relates right and wrong to individual taste. This is extreme relativism and sounds untenable when stated as baldly as in the previous sentence. However, evidence of this kind of thinking is common in our society. One sign is the emphasis on tolerance: "I have a right to my opinion and you have the right to yours." A second idea that reflects relativism is the acceptance of the inevitability of change. An inflexible adherence to the dogmas of the past is considered poor preparation for the future in a dynamic society.

One of the lessons to be learned in evaluation is that facts and values are not the same and should not be treated alike in reasoning. This lesson is most difficult for the person who holds values to be absolute and who has great confidence in the truth of his values. As a minimum, he must learn that intelligent people can sincerely hold other values than his own and that values cannot be proven to be true by logical or scientific processes.

The following form of question is helpful in leading students to distinguish between facts and values:

Which of the following are statements of fact and which are statements of values?

A. Washington, D. C., is located on the Potomac River.
B. A capital city should be located near the center of the nation.
C. Philadelphia was our national capital before Washington, D. C.
D. That government is best which governs least.

This type of exercise reveals that the dividing line between fact and value is not always clear.

All values are opinions in the sense that values cannot be proven to be true. However, all opinions are not values, because opinions often result from lack of access to information or take the form of predictions. This understanding can be developed by a question, such as the following:

Indicate whether each of the following is a "fact," "value," or an "opinion that is not a value."

A. Wars are bad.
B. The United States participated in two world wars in the first half of the twentieth century.
C. Neither the United States nor Russia will start a nuclear war, because the leaders of both realize that it would mean mutual destruction.
D. I'm willing to wager that if you check the record you will

find that the federal debt increased every year, except one, of the Eisenhower administration.

E. Economic freedom is the most important need of the American farmer.

Another understanding necessary for evaluation is that to assess the quality of something requires a knowledge of purpose. In judging the merits of a cow, it is necessary to know whether the animal is to provide milk or meat, be the subject for a painting, the advertising symbol of a milk company, or an object for worship.

After students are acquainted with the differences between fact, value, and opinion, and realize the need to consider purpose in evaluation, they are ready to begin practice in the first step— the setting of standards. Questions such as the following are appropriate:

Directions: Establish a purpose and appropriate standards for evaluating each of the following: (A) *a policeman;* (B) *a school library;* (C) *a neighborhood;* (D) *a national economic system;* (E) *a world government.* These sample problems show that the difficulty of the question is related to the complexity of the idea to be evaluated.

The next questions test skill in using the second step in measuring the ideas or things to be evaluated against the standards or values established:

1. A corporation is seeking a location for a new factory. The officers make the following list of characteristics of the city that would meet their needs. To what extent does our community meet the requirements? You will have to find information in the library and make inquiries in the community to answer the question.

   A. Access to rail transportation to all parts of the nation
   B. Availability of laborers skilled in metal work
   C. Low state and local taxes

D. A forty-acre building site on the edge of the community
E. An ample supply of coal either mined locally or delivered at low cost by water transportation
F. Availability of 1000 gallons of fresh but not purified water each day
G. A community with a history of good relations between management and labor

2. Mr. X believes that any law should meet these standards:
    A. Not increase the power of the federal government at the expense of the state and local goverments
    B. Not increase government debt
    C. Not undermine citizens' character by giving them something for nothing
    D. Not restrict the honest operation of business and industry
    E. Not be inflationary.

If Mr. X used only these standards, how would he rate the following laws?
    A. Sherman Anti-trust Act, 1890
    B. McKinley Tariff, 1890
    C. Pure Food and Drug Act, 1906
    D. Mann-Elkins Act, 1910
    E. Federal Reserve Act, 1913.

Examples of Evaluation Questions

1. An example of evaluation is found in an article in *The English Journal* entitled "A Question of Values: A Unit in Written Composition."[3] The authors pose a hypothetical question in which eleven people find themselves in a bomb shelter after a nuclear

[3] Patricia Klemans and Elizabeth Beidler, "A Question of Values: A Unit in Written Composition," *The English Journal*, September, 1962, pp. 421–423.

attack with oxygen and other supplies necessary to provide for only six people. The owner of the shelter must decide which five people should leave in order to save the others. A description of each individual is offered to help the student arrive at an answer. The basic problem is to set standards defining who most deserves to be saved and then to measure each individual against these standards.

2. The consideration of controversial issues often falls in the evaluation category, because they reflect differences of opinion on values. Most teachers are aware of the need to see that all sides of controversial issues are fully and fairly presented. However, two important aspects of such instruction are frequently ignored. First, students are often unaware of the intellectual process of evaluation. They confuse facts with values, argue from unrecognized and often contradictory value patterns, and presume that their opponents are stupid because they cannot follow "plain logic." Second, most controversial issues argued heatedly represent thinking only slightly above the memory level. This is usually true when considering old standard issues or in instances of current issues widely covered in the news; because, when students gather information on the problem, they also find a complete evaluation made by experts. All that students must do is choose the experts with whom they agree and recite their arguments in the discussion. This is a low level of evaluation, but it is the level on which most citizens make their decisions on public issues. The "old chestnut" issues, such as the need for federal aid to education, the proper interpretation of the separation of church and state, and the power of labor unions, are worthy of study in the classroom on the memory level because of the importance of the knowledge. In addition to these, students should consider contemporary issues in which they must make the evaluations. This can be arranged by submitting controversies on which expert evaluation is not likely to be available to them.

3. Some of the better students are ready to begin a relatively sophisticated level of evaluation before they leave high school.

One approach that has worked well in eleventh-grade American history and twelfth-grade problems of democracy centers around small reading-discussion groups. Six to eight students are invited to participate in the project for one marking period (about six weeks). The criteria for their selection are standardized achievement test scores in social studies and reading, plus scholastic aptitude scores, teacher judgment, and interest on the part of the student. The program consists of reading and evaluating one book each week. A student in the reading group does not attend his regular social studies class but reports to the school library each day for that period. All students in a group read the same book each week. Paperback copies are used, so that it is possible for the school to purchase one for each student. The books cover the general topic that the regular classes are studying. For example, during a unit on comparative political systems, the reading groups have studied books, such as these: *The United States Political System and How It Works* by David Cushman Coyle; *The Last Hurrah* by Edwin O'Connor; *Advise and Consent* by Allen Drury; *The Republic* by Charles A. Beard; *The Making of the President, 1960* by Theodore H. White; *The Animal Farm* and *Nineteen Eighty-four* by George Orwell; *Inside Europe Today* by John Gunther; *Looking Backward* by Edward Bellamy. After reading the weekly book, students write evaluations. On one evening each week they meet for a one- to two-hour discussion of the assigned book. The primary objective is to give students practice in evaluating the ideas in the book. In an introductory meeting the teacher stresses the difference between a summary and an evaluation of a book. The questions below are submitted to the students as a guide to different kinds of evaluation. They are placed in rough order of difficulty:

A. Is the book well written from a literary standpoint?
B. Is the author qualified to write on the subject? Is he likely to be biased? What does the book reveal of the author's personality?

C. Is the information in the book accurate? Does it agree with knowledge you already have on the subject or knowledge you can find in other sources?

D. Are the assumptions or conclusions of the book subject to controversy? What are other positions taken on the same issues?

E. Is the logic of the book sound? Are the main conclusions reached inductively or deductively? Did the author misuse either process? Did you find the use of logical fallacies? (These questions are not useful unless the teacher and students have had previous instruction in the elementary ideas in formal logic.)

F. What philosophical foundations underlie the book? What is the author's concept of man's nature and destiny? Does he treat truth as being absolute or relative? How does he believe truth to be discovered? What is the author's idea of the relationship between means and ends?

When students make their first evaluations, they tend to emphasize questions A, B, C. When attempting to deal with the other questions, they frequently make sweeping statements without specific confirmation. The teacher can lead students to more skill with the last three questions by demonstrating their application in the discussion.

Many students feel unqualified to make the judgments necessary in evaluation. This is good, because, in truth, they *are* unqualified. However, they must see that skill in evaluation develops with practice and that everyone must start on a low level of proficiency. The objective of the teacher is to maintain the students' humility, but, at the same time, to encourage them to try out a new intellectual experience.

4. Evaluation questions are fairly common among suggestions at the chapter endings in textbooks. Following are examples:

Harold H. Eibling *et al., Our Country's Story* (River Forest, Illinois: Laidlaw Brothers, 1958).

A. Each pupil could write a paragraph about your [*sic*.] favorite man or woman in Unit I. Tell why this person is your favorite. (p. 70.) [This kind of question based on personal whim should not be used very often.]

B. You could have a panel discussion on this subject, "Are wars necessary?" (p. 262.)

Prudence Cutright and John Jarolimek (eds.), *Living As World Neighbors* (New York: Macmillan, 1962).

A. Which country—Greece or England—in your opinion developed ideas that have been the most valuable to us? (p. 69.)

B. For many years Great Britain guarded the Suez Canal under an International Commission. In 1956 Egypt took control of the waterway. Do you think the canal should be operated by a single country? Or would it be better for a world organization, such as the United Nations, to manage the canal? Give reasons for your opinion. (p. 299.)

C. Would you favor strict laws requiring all farmers to practice soil conservation? Give reasons for your answer. (p. 463.)

Thomas A. Bailey, *The American Pageant Quiz Book* (Boston: Heath, 1961).

A. Argue all sides of the proposition that it would have been better for all concerned if Negro slavery had never been introduced into America. (p. 2.)

B. Was it a blunder for the British to deprive France of Canada in 1763? (p. 10.)

C. Argue both sides of the proposition that the Federalists did more harm than good during their life as a party. (p. 35.)

D. Argue both sides of the proposition that the British were justified in practicing impressment as they did. (p. 38.)

E. How would you rate the importance of the following people in the purchase of Louisiana: Jefferson, Monroe, Livingston, Napoleon, L'Ouverture, John Adams? Explain your listing. (p. 38.)

F. Who in your judgment was the most important literary figure in the United States before 1860? Defend your choice. (p. 70.)

G. Should fanatics like Garrison, who stirred up so much trouble, be allowed to speak freely, or should they be locked up in institutions for the good of society? (p. 74.)

H. In the light of what happened, is William Garrison to be regarded as a hero or a villain in American history? Explain fully. (p. 75.)

I. Was it wrong of the North to appease the South in 1850 with the Fugitive Slave Law? Discuss. (p. 78.)

J. Was Cleveland courageous or just bull-headed? (p. 102.)

K. Were the great industrial figures of the late 19th Century "robber barons" or "industrial statesmen"? (p. 106.)

In conclusion, evaluation is among the most difficult of mental activities, because there can be no absolute assurance that the product represents truth. The authors of the text, *Applied Logic*, comment on this aspect of evaluation:

It does not follow . . . that we should avoid making or using value judgments because they cannot be proved. . . . The man who has not answered for himself the question of what constitutes the highest good in life cannot run his life intelligently. . . . Value judgments are so important that we should apply all available techniques to the problem of finding those with the highest possible reliability.[4]

QUESTIONS ON CHAPTER EIGHT

1._____ Which of the following most accurately and completely describes the thinking process of the evaluation category? (A) Correcting objective test papers and assign grades; (B) Judging something after having set appropriate values; (C) Determining the truth of a matter; (D) Setting standards of right or wrong.

2._____ Which of the following is *not* an understanding that students should master before they are ready to answer evaluation questions? (A) In evaluation, the first step is to identify appropriate standards or values for the idea or object being judged. (B) To evaluate an idea or object properly requires knowledge of its proposed use. (C) The last step in evaluation is to decide whether the idea or object to be judged is an opinion or a fact. (D) Values cannot be proven true in the sense

[4] Winston Little *et al.*, *Applied Logic* (Boston: Houghton Mifflin, 1955), p. 261.

that is possible with facts. (E) All the above should be understood by students.

3._____ True or False: The answer to an evaluation question is always at least partly subjective.

4._____ True or False: All evaluation questions are moral or ethical problems.

5._____ True or False: Values cannot be proven to be true.

6._____ True or False: Some values are much more controversial than others.

7. Creativity is to _____ as judgment is to evaluation. (Fill in the blank.)

8. Of all seven categories of questions, which two most clearly lead to subjective answers?

9. Place a check before each of the following questions that exhibits the characteristics of evaluation:

_____A. Does the taxonomy of questions provide a good tool for improving the quality of education? Tell why.

_____B. Write a series of evaluation questions.

_____C. In what way are synthesis and evaluation questions similar?

_____D. Discuss the truth of this statement: Good teachers use a variety of questions.

_____E. What are the characteristics of evaluation?

10. Classify each of the following questions as memory, translation, interpretation, application, analysis, synthesis, or evaluation. (Assume that the person answering the questions has read all chapters through evaluation.) You may qualify any answer that you wish.

_____A. What are three uses a teacher could make of the taxonomy of questions?

_____B. True or False: The concept of evaluation is an inductive generalization.

_____C. Discuss this statement: The most important category of questions is evaluation.

_____D. Which idea does not fit in this list? (A) remember; (B) restate in other terms or symbols; (C) relate; (D) use in lifelike situations; (E) make a mistake; (F) create; (G) judge.

_____E. Which of the three systems of values do you believe to be best? Defend your answers.

11. Write your own list of characteristics of evaluation questions to serve as a reference.
12. Write five or more evaluation questions.

ANSWERS TO QUESTIONS ON
CHAPTER EIGHT

1. B.
2. C.   The last step in evaluation is to measure that which is being evaluated against the appropriate values or standards.
3. True.
4. False.
5. True.
6. True.
7. Synthesis.
8. Synthesis and evaluation.
9. A and D should be checked.
10. A. Memory; (Uses of the taxonomy are listed in Chapter One and therefore could be remembered. However, a reader might have composed a new use which represents thinking as high as the synthesis category.)   B. Interpretation; (The solution requires remembering the nature of an inductive generalization and the characteristics of evaluation. A comparison of the two reveals that they are not the same.)   C. Evaluation;   D. Interpretation;   E. Evaluation.

NINE

❖

PLANNING FOR QUESTIONING

Choosing a Level of Commitment

A TEACHER composes or selects questions for instruction and evaluation nearly every day. The most modest commitment to the taxonomy would lead him to keep the seven basic kinds of questions in mind while performing this normal function. However, some teachers prefer more deliberate planning. This begins with a consideration of the forms of thinking that are appropriate for the course and a decision to place new emphasis on certain kinds of questions. For example, the teacher with a special interest in the transfer of training might decide to experiment with the use of more application questions by selecting important definitions, generalizations, and skills, and plotting strategy for their use on the application level. Another system is to plan special lessons to develop an important skill or concept. If the idea of "cause and effect" is selected as the focus for several lessons, students can learn to relate this functional idea to the subject matter of the course. Broad concepts such as geographical determinism, social class, or standard of living, can be developed into beautiful lessons introducing important ideas that are to be followed up by interpretation and application questions in subsequent units.

A variation in the use of the taxonomy is to compose a unit focusing on neglected categories of thinking. The decision to do this should be made well in advance of the schedule for instruction in order to give sufficient time for preparation. Several eighth-grade United States history teachers decided in January to compose such a unit on the Civil War to be taught in May. They jointly planned the procedures and then individually worked out special lessons that were made available to all.

The ultimate commitment to the taxonomy of questions is the long-range program of building an entire course with a conscious consideration of the thought processes of students. This is normally undertaken by teachers who have had earlier success with special lessons or units. A reasonable rule of thumb for an academic course is that a minimum of one-third of the time allotted to questioning in both instruction and evaluation should be devoted to levels above memory. Some units lend themselves to a greater proportion of questions above this level, but it is difficult to justify a smaller proportion in any unit. The reason that time, rather than the number of questions, is used as the unit of measure is that questions in the upper categories often take longer to answer, so that ten memory questions may fill the same amount of time as one or two on a higher level.

In applying the ideas in this book a teacher should not expect questions of high quality to flow as water from a fountain. Good questions are difficult to compose. Sometimes a carefully formulated series of questions does not bring the expected responses from the pupils. In this case the teacher studies the questions to determine whether they are too difficult, improperly constructed, or if additional instruction should have been offered to prepare the students for the questions. He discards questions that cannot be repaired and saves the good ones. This means that each year the teacher starts with a larger stock of questions. The more experience he has in composing and using questions, the easier the process becomes.

Suggestions for Composing Questions

Before a teacher writes a unit, a lesson, or even a single question, he should steep himself in the subject, with his mind attuned to possible intellectual experiences for his students. In teaching on the memory level, a teacher need not know much more subject matter than is found in the students' textbooks. With higher categories of thinking, this is not true. The teacher must have a deep mastery of his subject and read widely in his field to keep abreast of new knowledge and interpretations. A teacher who knows only one example of the operation of a difficult principle can use it in instruction but then must revert to the memory level for evaluation. A teacher who knows two examples of the operation of a principle can use one in instruction and one on the interpretation or application level in evaluating student progress. A teacher who knows five examples of the operation of a principle can both instruct and evaluate student progress on the interpretation or application level. This teacher may find one of the five examples is best for slow learners and another for the gifted. The point is that the more knowledge a teacher has, the better chance he has to fashion learning on all levels appropriate for his students.

Another advantage of scholarship is that it gives a teacher more confidence in subjective evaluation. The teacher who avoids the synthesis and evaluation categories is often the one who has not had enough experience in his subject field to be able to give a convincing judgment of the quality of a student's work.

While studying a topic in preparation for instruction, the teacher should be on the lookout for the big working ideas—the generalizations, values, definitions, and skills that are important enough to deserve emphasis. These are the ideas that best lead to higher level questions. In considering them, it is wise to think of the process whereby the knowledge came into man's possession and then determine whether students could profitably retrace any of these steps if given the background.

Textbooks create a major problem for teachers concerned with composing good questions. Although many are attractive, accurate, readable, and understandable, they are also one of the biggest deterrents to thinking in the classroom, because the writers assume that students learn best by studying a polished product. The key function of the writer is to explain, and a good explanation is interesting, orderly, accurate, and complete. The vocabulary suits the level of the student and complex ideas are clarified by dissection, integration, example, and visual images. *Thus, the textbook is weak in that it offers little opportunity for any mental activity except remembering.* If there is an inference to be drawn, the author draws it, and if there is a significant relationship to be noted, the author points it out. There are no loose ends or incomplete analyses. The textbook is highly refined and as near perfection as a human mind is capable of making it —but the author does the thinking. The book never gives a clue that the author pondered (maybe even agonized) over hundreds of decisions. The result is that the creative process and the controversy of competing ideas are hidden from the students.

Suggested questions and activities at the end of the chapter vary in quality from book to book. Even in the best, the questions that go beyond memory are too often on peripheral matters or on controversial issues, which are safer to present in question form than to discuss in the text.

Students deserve the right to participate in the thinking. They deserve the right to reason with raw, undigested ideas. They are not ready to take over *all* the thinking functions of the writers, but they can take over *part* of them. To accomplish this in a text, the author might stop his explanatory function at various points and, in effect, say to the student: "The next idea to be developed is one you can think out if I give you the raw material. This is an important idea and will be used later in the text. Give it your serious thought."

To put the emphasis on thinking into practice in a classroom, *a teacher must present subject matter from sources in addition to the text.* He must develop a sensitivity to ideas that are useful in instruction and evaluation. Pertinent ideas take such forms as these:

1. A contradiction to information offered in the text
2. A different interpretation or evaluation than offered in the text
3. Additional evidence to support a point made in the text
4. A different line of reasoning to arrive at a conclusion made in the text
5. A new example of the use of a generalization, value, definition, or skill developed in the text
6. More recent or accurate information on a topic presented in the text

Good thought-provoking questions almost jump out of these kinds of ideas. For example, if a teacher finds "a different line of reasoning to arrive at a conclusion made in the text," he can use the following approach: After giving students the new line of reasoning, but not the conclusion, he asks: "What conclusion follows from these ideas? What form of thinking was used to reach this conclusion? By what other line of reasoning can the same conclusion be reached? Which set of arguments best supports the conclusion? Is there any other approach to establishing the same conclusion?"

The information from sources other than the textbook can be offered to students in a number of ways. It can be presented orally or printed in mimeographed form. If possible, it should be directly quoted; but, if the vocabulary is inappropriate, the teacher may paraphrase the ideas. New duplicating equipment enables one to make a ditto master directly from a printed page, so that in a few minutes a teacher (or secretary) can ditto copies of an article for every member of a class. Pictures, graphs, and statistics can be transmitted to students by making slides or transparencies for an overhead projector. This problem of getting information to students is mechanical but must not be ignored, because the whole process of questioning depends on the proper flow of ideas into the classroom.

Paperback books offer opportunities for bringing provocative ideas to the students. The large number of titles and the low cost mean that a school system can afford supplementary books on many units. When the teacher finds a paperback that raises possibilities for good thinking, he can order enough copies for reference reading in the school library and then plan for the kind of questions that will fruitfully follow. The school system that encourages teaching on this level should provide teachers with materials and opportunities for study and thinking.

A vital point to remember in planning questions is that almost any important concept can be taught in several ways that will lead the students to different levels of thinking.[1] The teacher's problem is to select the procedure that is most appropriate. For example, suppose an eleventh-grade American history teacher wishes to teach the concept that wages of city working men were on the average increasing faster between 1865 and 1900 than were prices of consumer goods, and this relationship, plus the increasing production of consumer goods and the low level of taxes, led to a modest improvement in the standard of living of the city workers. Three variations of strategy of instruction are suggested below:

1. The teacher explains the relationships among wages, prices, production, taxes, and standard of living. He then asks the stu-

---

[1] One illustration of this is the three approaches to instruction of the concept of "conflict of interest" which are offered in the questions at the end of Chapter One.

dents to recite the same information in class and later to write it
on an essay or objective test.

2. The teacher presents statistical or graphic data on wages,
prices, production, and taxes of the period from 1860 to 1900 and
asks students to draw generalizations about the trends in each
and to speculate on what was happening to the workers' standard
of living.[2]

3. The teacher presents one of many statements describing the
view that industrial robber barons of the 1865–1900 period ex-
ploited the city workers. The statistical evidence on wages, prices,
production, and taxes could then be offered with the problem of
determining whether or not this data substantiated the interpretation.

There are many more variations for the instruction of this one
lesson. The teacher must choose the one he feels best suits the
situation. To make this decision, he considers such things as the
ability and motivation of the students, the time available, and the
objectives of the course. For example, if course objectives call for
emphasis on recent United States history, then the first approach
is best in speeding the progress through the post-Civil War unit.
If course objectives stress concentration on economic concepts or
on skill in using statistical data, then the second or third approach
seems best. If objectives stress the need for students to understand that historians interpret history and often disagree, then the
last approach should be chosen.

In constructing questions in the higher categories, teachers
should remember that there are likely to be several points in the
thinking in which a student might make an error. A student could
fail to answer an application question properly because of inability to remember necessary information or inability to translate
the problem into a familiar context. Sometimes a teacher may
wish to de-emphasize the memory aspects of a problem, so that

[2] This information is available from the following sources: U. S. Department of Commerce, *Historical Statistics of the United States*
(Washington, D.C.: U.S. Government Printing Office, 1960).

he knows a mistake reflects a breakdown in thinking on a higher level. This procedure is easily accomplished by providing all necessary information in the problem or by giving an "open-book" and "open-notes" test. For example, a unit in a Problems of Democracy course dealt with taxation and included an exercise on filling out federal income-tax forms. An obvious question for instruction and evaluation was to ask students to make out forms for mythical individuals. In composing the examination, the question arose as to whether students should be allowed to use the instruction booklet available to taxpayers to check on processes, kinds of deductions, etc. The answer—that students should be able to use all these materials because memorizing this information is not necessary, even for taxpayers—seemed obvious. This de-emphasis on memory should not carry to all application questions, because in many situations in life the use of skills in solving problems is dependent on the ability to remember necessary information.

The last suggestion in this section deals with a differentiation made between questions for instruction and those for evaluation leading to grading. In the memory category, the same questions serve both functions. With questions above the memory level, a complication arises in that the second time a question is asked, it can be answered by memory. An important rule in framing questions is that questions designed for grading should reflect the same kind of thinking used in instruction. It is wrong to ask a variety of levels of questions in instruction but revert to the memory category in evaluation. It is equally wrong to conduct instruction on the memory level in order to save higher level questions for an examination. The best way to avoid these errors is to compose examination questions and instructional questions at the same time and make a determined effort to keep them parallel.

The preceding suggestions for composing questions are summarized in the following points:

1. The greater depth a teacher has in a topic, the more poten-

tial he has for writing a variety of good questions. When preparing a lesson or a unit, a teacher should look for the kinds of ideas that are important and susceptible to use in thinking.

2. Textbooks help a teacher present an orderly sequence of subject matter but are written in a manner that encourages only the use of memory. Higher level questions often require the withholding of conclusions drawn in the text until the students have had an opportunity to do some thinking. Questions in the higher categories frequently require sources of information in addition to the text.

3. Almost any idea or skill can be taught in several ways featuring different kinds of thinking. The teacher should be aware of all possibilities and choose the most appropriate according to his objectives.

4. Questions classified in the higher categories can be missed by students on lower intellectual levels. For example, an application question may be missed because of inability to remember, translate, or interpret information. Teachers should bear this in mind when ascertaining the causes of errors in students' solutions.

5. Questions used to evaluate student progress should call for the same kinds of thinking as those used in instruction. It is not right to instruct on the level of higher categories of thinking and then evaluate only the ability to remember.

The Proper Format for Short-Answer and Discussion Questions

The format of a question is a vital consideration, because a potentially good question in any category of thinking can be ruined by improper construction. The most common forms of short-answer questions are true-false, completion, matching, and multiple-choice. Short-answer questions are often called "objective," but this distinction requires a reservation. An objective question asks for one specific answer that can be recognized as correct or incorrect by any person knowledgeable on the subject. It does not require an expression of individual feelings and opinions. A short-answer question should be objective, but the form of the question does not guarantee that there is only one correct answer. A faultily constructed short-answer question may allow for several interpretations because of ambiguity or because it asks for evaluation or synthesis without offering the opportunity to carry out the entire process. Nothing is more frustrating for a student than to be confronted with a question that can be answered in several ways but offers only the opportunity to choose one answer with no qualifications. One objective of this book is to encourage teachers to use more subjective questions but not in the objective format.

The advantages of short-answer questions are that they can be used to instruct and evaluate diverse kinds and amounts of subject matter and skills, and are easy to correct. Teachers like them because they offer a precise scale for grading that discourages quibbling. The disadvantages are that they take a long time to compose in volume and are easily subject to errors in construction. Following are suggestions for composing short-answer questions:

1. Do not write questions on trivial ideas.
2. Do not use vague language, as in this example:
   "True or False: China is larger than the Soviet Union." The wording does not establish whether area or population is to be compared.
3. Make certain the question calls for a single, correct response.
4. In composing true-false questions:
   A. Remember the law of averages enters heavily into the score on these questions; so include enough items to establish reliability.
   B. Do not overuse superlatives as they usually indicate the answer is false.

C. Do not yield to the temptation of making true questions consistently longer than false questions:

5. In composing completion questions:

   A. Make certain that only one response is correct.

   B. Do not put in so many blanks that the question loses meaning.

   C. Do not permit the syntax of the statement or the length of the blank to give a hint as to the answer.

6. In composing matching questions:

   A. Do not include heterogeneous subjects that reveal answers by extraneous clues.

   B. Include more items in the response column, so that the last questions cannot be answered by elimination.

7. In composing multiple-choice questions:

   A. Include at least four options, but do not use obviously phony ones.

   B. Use "None of the above" or "All of the above" as a final option when appropriate.

   C. Include enough questions to raise reliability.

   D. Keep all options grammatically consistent.[3]

Short-answer questions can lead to thinking in all categories except synthesis and evaluation. However, full exploration of all categories requires additional use of discussion questions.

A discussion question is one in which a student is called upon to present an oral or written answer of a sentence or more in his own words. Some discussion questions calling for only a sentence or two are quite objective in the sense that they ask for specific information that is easily judged right or wrong. Examples would be questions asking for a simple definition or identification. Longer, more involved discussion questions are always at least

---

[3] For excellent suggestions on the format of questions, see James Bradfield and H. Stewart Moredock, *Measurement and Evaluation in Education* (New York: Macmillan Co., 1957); N. M. Downie, *Fundamentals of Measurement* (New York: Oxford University Press, 1958).

somewhat subjective—even when stressing the memorization of information—because of the problem of determining the amount of substantiation and description necessary to answer the questions.

The advantages of discussion questions are that they are fairly easy to compose and can be used to lead students into every category of the taxonomy. They also require students to organize and express ideas in their own words.

The disadvantages of discussion questions lie in the difficulty of evaluating them fairly. Educational research offers ample evidence that evaluation of subjective answers is a precarious process. A group of teachers correcting the same essays assign a great range of grades. A teacher correcting the same set of papers twice, with an interval of time between, usually makes different evaluations the second time. The uneasy feeling in correcting essay answers, the difficulty of justifying evaluations to students, and the great amount of time required to correct them all conspire to force teachers to neglect or misuse them. This is unfortunate, as it denies students practice in important kinds of thinking. A better approach is to reduce some of the disadvantages and to learn to live with the others. Specific suggestions follow:

1. Do not use essay questions to evaluate knowledge that could be tested with objective questions. For the most part, purely memory questions should not be in essay form. Seldom need a test be wholly in essay form, because objective questions are appropriate for many categories. This allows the teacher opportunity to do a better job in correcting a smaller number of subjective answers.

2. Before correcting the responses to a subjective question, think out as many approaches as possible. Decide on elements that appear to be essential in the various approaches. On some subjective questions, the answers are not dependent so much on the evaluation the student makes as on how well he supports his position.

3. Write comments and corrections on essay responses, be-

cause they are more revealing than a single grade. This is a time-consuming task and accentuates the need to keep the volume of reading within reasonable limits. One essay answer carefully corrected is worth two or three read in a cursory manner and assigned a grade with no explanation.

4. Make a point not to know whose paper is being read when correcting. It is too easy to get a stereotyped evaluation in mind for each student and unconsciously give the accustomed grade. Anonymity can easily be attained by having the name folded under a corner of the paper or written in an inconspicuous place.

5. Compose a guide for answering essay questions and go over it with students at the beginning of the year. Here is an example:

A. Survey the entire test quickly, noting the directions and estimating the importance and difficulty of each question.

B. Apportion the time available among the questions so that you will be able to answer adequately all required questions during the period. Allow more time for important or difficult questions. Plan to use all of the time available. Allow time at the end of the period for proofreading. Keep to your plan for the division of time.

C. Analyze each question carefully. Decide what is called for and what is *not* called for in your answer. The key nouns in the question will suggest the topic and subtopics for your essay. Verbs (compare, contrast, explain, discuss, define, describe, summarize, etc.) will tell you how to approach the topic. Phrases such as "before 1917" or "in the U.S.S.R." suggest limitations of the topic.

D. Organize each answer before you begin to write. Decide what important ideas are required according to your anlysis of the question. Jot down notes on the important ideas and organize them in a pattern. (The question itself will often suggest an organization for the answer.) Outline the pattern of ideas and add specific points under each. Good organization shortens writing time and makes the answer more clear.

E. Write each answer, following your outline and remembering the analysis of the question. Use proper form, grammar, and punctuation. Avoid repetition and unnecessary phrases. Avoid long introductions and conclusions.

F. Additional hints: Define key terms. Use technical terms and new vocabulary you have learned. Be as specific as possible. Distinguish between theory and fact. Cite authority whenever you can. Identify opinion. Use your reasoning power as well as your memory. Do not hesitate to be original in approach and interpretation.

G. A good answer to an essay question will (1) show understanding of the question and all its implications, (2) show adequate knowledge of fact and theory related to the question, (3) exclude irrelevant material, (4) be well organized with emphasis placed upon more important ideas, (5) demonstrate ability to write clearly, (6) contain valid reasoning, and (7) include originality when appropriate to the question.

Another opportunity to give students practice in answering both short-answer and discussion questions is in classroom recitation. A good oral discussion question is subject to several avenues of attack by individuals who have differing backgrounds and temperaments. In participating in an oral discussion, students exhibit most of the same kinds of thinking necessary in writing the answer to an essay question. The educational value of classroom recitation can be augmented by evaluating the contributions of the members of the class. One system involving some bookkeeping but that has proven to work well is to have the teacher evaluate student participation during the course of the recitation. He has a seating chart before him and records credit for every student response according to a simple system, such as this:

1. Adequate answer to a simple factual memory question: one point

2. Adequate answer to a more complicated question: two or three points
3. Adequate answer to a simple translation or interpretation question: three or four points
4. Adequate answer to an application, analysis, synthesis or evaluation question: five to ten points
5. Student asks a pertinent question: four or five points

The amount of credit a student attains within each range is dependent upon the difficulty of the question and the quality of the response. With practice, a teacher can use this system without slowing down the flow of questions. The students are told about the system and know their recitation will account for one-fourth of their grades. This has a motivational influence on oral work and offers a way to present more subjective questions to the class in a manner that counts in the grade. The teacher is also able to present a mixture of objective and subjective questions, of easy and difficult questions, to the appropriate students.

Mistakes to Avoid

As with any idea in education, a special concern for questions poses certain dangers. Teachers who strive for higher level questions may lose interest in the bread-and-butter memory question. They become so intrigued with sending students through intellectual labyrinths that they neglect fundamental knowledge. They may tend to cater to the capacities of superior students. Simple questions designed for slow students are just as necessary as complex ones in all categories. Subjective questions are important and have a challenge of their own but should be mixed with a liberal number of objective ones. There is satisfaction in giving the one right answer to an objective question and being told the response is correct.

The teacher must be careful to maintain continuity in instruction and to make certain that students see the logical organization of the instruction. One advantage of following a textbook is that, at any point in the course, the student can ascertain what has been covered and where the instruction is heading. The approach to instruction advocated in these pages urges teachers not to lean too heavily on the text; to present more information than is included in the book; to present other points of view; and to avoid using only the text on some topics in order to control the sequence of ideas to students. This places an extra responsibility on teachers to make certain that the instruction does not appear disjointed. Students should be required to save their notes and exercises worked out in class for review purposes. A written outline of the sequence of topics may be necessary for students to envision the direction and progress of the unit.

It takes longer for students to think their way through a unit than it does for them to memorize the thinking of others. This intensifies the difficulty of finding time to cover the significant topics in the course of the year. Even if time were not a factor, it would be unwise to have students try to figure out everything. In any unit, the teacher must determine the most lucrative areas for higher-category questions and judge the amount of time that can reasonably be devoted to them. Any substantial switch from memory to higher categories in a course requires some reduction in the amount of subject matter that can be considered. This can be justified only because it makes room for an increase in the practice of valuable intellectual skills.

The main caution to teachers who are undertaking to apply the taxonomy of questions is to keep the enterprise in proper perspective. A variety of questions at all costs is an untenable approach. Intellectual gymnastics do not strengthen the brain; but clearly defined intellectual skills applied to significant subject matter do prepare students for similar problems in life. The following selection illustrates the final point in this chapter that *good* questions can be ludicrous when applied to insignificant subject matter:

"This Little Pig went to market."

Why? Did he go to buy or to be bought? Is he a free agent? If to buy, what and for whom? Is he an informed buyer, the sort who would study the Buyers' Index and Consumers' Guide? If, and it is altogether possible, if he is to be sold, what price will he bring? What will be the effect on the market price of the recent attempts to control agricultural surplus? And, in our ever-widening circle of relationships, is there a reasonable or an exorbitant profit for the farmer?

"This Little Pig stayed home."

Once again, why? Why did he stay home? Was he perhaps antisocial? What was there in his background that caused him to stay home? What was his home like? What did he do there? He may have been a truant. What can we do to make our schools attractive to the potential truant? Is it good for us to stay home sometimes?

"This Little Pig had roast beef."

Would you consider roast beef proper food for a pig? Which is better, nutritionally speaking, rare or well-done meat?

"This Little Pig had none."

Why not? Did he eat something else? What would you suggest as a well-balanced diet for a pig? What bad psychological effects are likely to result from the juxtaposition of plenty and scarcity? One authority suggests that this little pig was suffering from some slight indisposition. Another suggests that he was being punished. Do you concur with either of these theories? Or was he on one of those liquid diets?

"This Little Pig cried 'Wee, Wee, Wee' all the way home."

Where had the little pig been? Why did he cry? What does this tell us about the pig's personality and character development? At what age do pigs change from "wee" to "oink"?

Let us now invite the children to participate in certain worthwhile activities which will provide experiential enrichment, accommodate individual differences, and permit the less literary and less articulate child to share in a rich experience.

1. Arrange a bulletin board on the theme, "Pigs in Literature." This can entail some research and should include of course, "Dissertation on Roast Pig," "Pigs Is Pigs," etc.

2. Build a home where a pig would like to stay. What size and shape would you make it? What materials and colors are most suitable?

3. Stay home yourself and see how you like it.

4. Prepare a scientific diet for a pig. Write to the U.S. Department of Agriculture, Washington 16, D.C., for the most recent information on the subject. Give careful attention to calorie intake and the proper balance of protein, carbohydrates, and fats. Consider particularly the cholesterol level of the diet.

5. Dramatize "This Little Pig." This poem can be adapted to the "theatre-in-the-round" technique.

6. Consult the visual-aids catalogues published by the visual-aids department of your school and show a film on pork production. Especially recommended is the U.S. Department of Agriculture film strip #208, "Pork Production in the United States, 1959."

7. Try fasting when others are eating to learn how that little pig felt. List the advantages of fasting.

8. Get a litter of five pigs and raise them so that they will be happy, healthy, and well adjusted. Keep a day-by-day account of their development, noting particularly their stability of personality.[4]

DISCUSSION QUESTIONS ON CHAPTER NINE

These questions differ from those in previous chapters. Questions 1 and 2 are recommended as worthwhile exercises to perform. The rest of the questions present problems on which the reader probably will have initial reactions but on which final answers will have to await further experimentation.

1. Select a generalization, definition, value, or skill and describe several ways it might be taught in which students would engage in different kinds of thinking.

[4] Bernice Black, "For The Teacher Only," in Martin Levin's "Phoenix Nest," *Saturday Review*, August 11, 1962, p. 7.

2. Measure the quality of the format of the questions that you have used on a test against the standards set in this chapter.
3. Invent the format of a textbook that would give students a greater intellectual responsibility than simply being consumers of an author's ideas.
4. Is there value in having students learn the meaning of some or all the categories of thinking? Tell why.
5. What factors make a question easy or difficult to answer? Is there a method, other than trial and error, for determining the level of complexity of ideas and skills that students of a certain mental age can master?
6. The charge has been made that teachers fail to keep up with new developments in their subject fields. To the extent that this may be true, what could be done to give teachers more time and motivation to study?
7. How might the taxonomy of questions be used in an in-service training program?
8. How might imaginative questions be included in curriculum bulletins in ways that would be helpful to teachers?

assume the reality of the forces of the sentiment, but we have read and accepted the world simply in a first chapter.

5. Invent the forces of questions that would give students a more deliberate responsibility than simply being consumers of materials literally.

6. What matter it brings study we know the amount of some of all the categories of challenging analysis.

7. What factors make a question answer difficult to improve? Is there a method other than trial and error in determining the level of complexity of ideas and skills that students of a certain mental age possess?

8. The choice between head that becomes difficult to keep up with new developments in their subject fields. To the degree that this may be true, what could be done to free teachers from time and method is so tedious.

9. How would be extension of questions become a central learning process?

10. How might intuitive questions be judged? Might someone formulate criteria or ways that would be helpful to teachers?

INDEX

67 68 69 70   7 6